Positive Discipline in the School and Classroom Leaders' Guide: Resources and Activities

Teresa LaSala, Jody McVittie and Suzanne Smitha

Based on

Positive Discipline in the Classroom Teacher's Guide

Revised Edition 1997

Jane Nelsen and Lynn Lott

Based on
Positive Discipline in the Classroom Teacher's Guide
by Jane Nelsen and Lynn Lott © Copyright 1997

Published by Positive Discipline Association

Printed in the United States of America

ISBN 978-0-9860181-1-4

Dedicated to the community of committed educators working to build respectful schools, classrooms and communities.

"Research also shows that building a sense of community in schools is an integral part of creating a positive learning environment. Community building begins on the first day students and teachers come together. It is here that social and emotional learning can be integrated into classroom life. Here, social emotional learning is seen not as an add-on for the teacher but the way that relationships, routines, and procedures are established so everyone feels cared for, respected, and valued."

Jacqueline A. Norris, "Looking at Classroom Management Through a Social and Emotional Learning Lens" *Theory into Practice*, Volume 42: 4 2003, p 315

You manage things. You lead people.

- Grace Murray Hopper

Positive Discipline in the School and Classroom Leaders' Guide: Resources and Activities

Table of Contents

Acknowledgements

We are grateful for the work of Alfred Adler and Rudolf Dreikurs, whose passionate commitment to respect and dignity for all human beings continues to be radical work and provides a solid foundation for a better world.

We are deeply indebted to our master teachers, Jane Nelsen and Lynn Lott, for their vision for Positive Discipline in schools. They published the first PDC Teacher's Guide in 1992 and revised it three additional times before they invited us to write this series. The 1997 revision provided the basic ideas for most of the activities in this manual. Jane and Lynn's willingness to trust and allow us to revise and reformat their content enabled us to bring the activities up to date for this generation of teachers and students. Their generosity of spirit has empowered hundreds of passionate men and women to be able to take this material to their own communities around the world with the expectation that their work is honored and done well, but without expecting to be paid every time it is used. May what they have midwifed continue to grow for generations to come.

This manual would not be what it is without the incredible community of colleagues who keep this work alive and growing in so many different corners of the world. Many pieces of the manual come from you. You inspire us. The Positive Discipline Association is a vibrant group of people who share their ideas and generate activities at an astounding rate. We have made a sincere effort to give credit to those who have provided the framework for specific activities included in this manual. Many teachers over the years have made their own contributions to Positive Discipline in the Classroom and their ideas have also been passed down among us. We appreciate the contributions and support of all who have made this manual possible.

Special thanks also to Cheryl Erwin. Her deep knowledge and careful eyes for editing have helped shape and enhanced our work.

Our appreciation to Lisa Rooney for the cover design and to Beat Barblan for his support and professional advice.

We extend deep gratitude to our families who are our best teachers and continuously hold space for us to work toward becoming our best selves.

Foreword

When we wrote the book *Positive Discipline in the Classroom* and the Teacher's Guide for the two-day workshop, we had no idea it would have the impact it has had on so many people. We are especially humbled that the PDC work has attracted people like Teresa LaSala, Jody McVittie, and Suzanne Smitha and many others who have become passionate about this work. We appreciate their experience and expertise in working with teachers and administrators in countless schools and workshops, and that they brought their experience, expertise, and passion to the revision of the manual in the *Positive Discipline in the School and Classroom Teachers' Guide: Activities for Students*. Now this second manual includes pieces from our original work, augments it and takes it further into the world. That has been our dream all along.

Jane Nelsen

Lynn Lott

Introduction

Positive Discipline weaves the teaching of social-emotional skills and character development into the fabric of each and every school day. Adults model the skills they are teaching and integrate them into the discipline system used by the school. The result is a campus-wide approach for effective discipline and a school, which systematically and intentionally cultivates a positive school culture and climate.

Positive Discipline in the School and Classroom Leaders' Guide: Resources and Activities is the second in a series of manuals. It is written to share the collective experiences of the authors and many others using and teaching Positive Discipline with diverse communities and student populations in public, private and parochial schools. It is intended to be used as a companion to *Positive Discipline in the School and Classroom Teachers' Guide: Activities for Students* which focuses on activities that educators use with students in the classroom and in small groups.

The *Positive Discipline in the School and Classroom* series and *Positive Discipline in the Classroom, 4th Ed* by Jane Nelsen and Lynn Lott provide the materials to empower schools to develop and implement a comprehensive school process that teaches mutual respect, fosters academic excellence and teaches students the basic skills they need in a structured, experiential manner.

This manual, *Positive Discipline in the School and Classroom Leaders' Guide: Resources and Activities* manual has been organized to serve three primary purposes:

- To provide the materials used in the Positive Discipline in the Classroom professional development training workshops.[1]
- To provide a source of information and short activities that schools adopting Positive Discipline can use to review and improve their practices in the classroom and school.
- To provide activities and ideas for educators who have taken the Positive Discipline in the Classroom training and wish to begin to share the material and process with their own school community.

As interest is generated in your school community we recommend inviting a Certified Positive Discipline Trainer (CPDT) to provide a full training for your school. If you or colleagues from your school are interested in training your own staff, it is highly recommended that you become a certified trainer (CPDT) through the Positive Discipline Association.[2]

Social Skills Make a Difference

Numerous studies have demonstrated that a systematic approach to the intentional implementation of a social-emotional learning (SEL) program into a school offers significant benefits. A recent review of programs by Durlak, et al (2011)[2] showed that SEL programs:

[1,2] Positive Discipline in the Classroom workshops are offered around the world as open workshops and also as custom workshops requested by individual schools or districts.. Current schedules are posted at www.PositiveDisicpline.org.

[2] Durlak, J. A., Weissberg, R. P., Dymnicki, A. B, Taylor, R. D.,& Schellinger, K. B. (2011) The Impact of Enhancing Students' Social and Emotional Learning: A Meta-Analysis of School-Based Universal Interventions. *Child Development*, 82 (1), 405–432. A link to the full paper can be found at http//casel.org/why-it-matters/benefits-of-sel/

- Improve students' achievement test scores across the spectrum by an average of 11 percentile points.
- Are effective in both school and after-school settings and for students with and without behavioral and emotional problems.
- Are effective for racially and ethnically diverse students from urban, rural, and suburban settings across the K-12 grade range.
- Improve students' social-emotional skills, attitudes about self and others, connection to school, and positive social behavior; and reduce conduct problems and emotional distress.

The paper also noted that school-based programs are most effective when they are conducted by school staff (e.g., teachers and student support staff) and can be incorporated into routine educational practice. In addition, effective programs and approaches are sequenced, active, focused, and explicit (S.A.F.E.), meaning they:

- S: Use a ***S***equenced set of activities to achieve skill objectives;
- A: Use ***A***ctive forms of learning;
- F: Include at least one program component ***F***ocused on developing personal or social skills; and
- E: ***E***xplicitly target particular personal or social skills for development.

Like other effective programs, the Positive Discipline curriculum outlined in this manual is sequenced, active, focused and explicit.

Implementing the Positive Discipline Social-Emotional Curriculum

Changing the culture of a school does not happen overnight; in fact, it requires commitment, patience, education, and practice. The way adults respond to inappropriate student behavior is an important model for student conduct. In a Positive Discipline School, every adult:

- Understands that the quality of relationships and school climate are absolutely critical to successful student learning.
- Seeks to establish strong meaning and connection for students, families and staff in social and academic contexts.
- Implements principles of mutual respect and encouragement.
- Focuses on long-term solutions to misbehavior at individual, class and school- wide levels.
- Views mistakes as opportunities to learn, and misbehavior as opportunities to practice critical life skills.
- Questions the tradition of adult control, rewards and punishments.

The long-term strategies for successful implementation of the Whole School Positive Discipline Social- Emotional Curriculum include:

- Training all school staff;[3]
- A commitment to school-wide teaching of the full curriculum;
- Intentionally making a respectful climate and culture a school priority;
- Regular practice (for adults and students);

---

[3] The Positive Discipline Association maintains a network of certified trainers. (For more information see www.positivediscipline.org)

- The presence of an oversight team;
- The use of behavior and climate data as feedback;
- Incorporating the model into school-wide practices (student council and students solving school-wide problems); and
- Engaging the broader community, which includes parents and caregivers.

School-wide Discipline

Although incorporating social skills and character development training into a school has significant long-term positive impacts, it is only one component of a comprehensive Positive Discipline system. Developing a discipline program that is consistent *and* leaves enough flexibility to allow for consideration of the individual student requires thought and commitment on the part of the school's staff and administration. It is the foundation of a culture of respect within the school.

Engaging all staff, students and families in building a learning community that models mutual respect and fosters academic excellence for all students is a huge challenge and requires:

- A general consensus among the school staff that *discipline is about teaching and learning--not punishment.* This does not mean eliminating consequences for serious or dangerous misbehavior. Such consequences are critical to civil society. Rather, it means rethinking everything that occurs up to that point. It also means rethinking how we implement consequences for serious or dangerous misbehavior and the downstream results of those consequences, so that students develop a *stronger connection* to their school community, rather than being pushed away.
- A principal and leadership team who believe that *rethinking discipline assumptions and practices to create more responsible, resilient and successful students is a high priority.*
- A principal, leadership team and staff who are *committed to increasing cultural competence* and who foster engagement and curiosity around issues of race, culture, class and gender.
- A school staff that accepts that improving discipline practices and school climate is far more demanding than merely adopting a new program. Rather, it is a *core school improvement strategy owned and managed well by the principal and staff.*
- A school staff that accepts that *improving discipline practices and school climate takes time* and who are willing to stay the course for three years or longer.
- A *willingness to collect and use discipline data* (including race information).
- A school staff that understand that *fostering a community of mutual respect to enhance student learning is a process* that will gradually include a larger and larger segment of the broader school community.

How to Use This Manual

Positive Discipline in the School and Classroom Leaders' Guide: Resources and Activities manual has been organized to serve three primary purposes:

1. To provide the materials used in the Positive Discipline in the Classroom professional development training workshops.[4]
   - The manual will be used as a resource during the training.
   - Refer back to the manual to supplement and deepen learning after the workshop.

2. To provide a source of information and short activities schools adopting Positive Discipline can use to review and improve their practices in the classroom and school.
   - School Positive Discipline leadership teams can use this manual to create a sustainability plan that includes regular staff development.
   - Short activities provided in the manual during staff meetings or professional development will encourage the whole staff to continue their focus on Positive Discipline practices.

3. To provide activities and ideas for educators who have taken the Positive Discipline in the Classroom training and wish to begin to share the material and process with their own school community.
   - The "Framework for Getting Started" will assist in developing a plan to share the material with your administration and staff.
   - After working with your administration "You've Agreed to Give a Presentation" gives tips for sharing with colleagues.

Moving it forward

We challenge you to move Positive Discipline forward in your school:

- Share what you learn with your school administration.
- Model what you have learned in your classroom or work area.
- Practice and model class meetings with your students.
- Invite colleagues to learn with you.
- Model mistakes as opportunities to learn.
- When the opportunity arises, share short activities with your staff.
- Consider being trained as a Certified Positive Discipline trainer.

In closing

Moving through this material in a step-wise fashion will grow cooperative and respectful relationships in your school and classroom, which will make your school the amazing place you want it to be. *We hope you enjoy the journey as much as we have.*

[4,2] Positive Discipline in the Classroom workshops are offered around the world as open workshops and also as custom workshops requested by individual schools or districts.. Current schedules are posted at www.PositiveDisicpline.org.

Positive Discipline Theory

A quick summary:

Positive Discipline is based on the work of Alfred Adler (1870-1937) and Rudolf Dreikurs (1897-1972), both Viennese psychiatrists. Adler's theory and practice were influenced by living in a poor neighborhood in highly class-structured society, by his indigent patients and his traumatic experience as a psychiatrist for the Austrian Army during World War I. After the war, Adler initiated a series of child guidance clinics to teach parents and teachers more effective methods for working with young people, using the democratic principles of dignity and respect. He believed that children needed both order (structure and responsibility) and freedom in order to grow into responsible, contributing citizens of their community. Dreikurs was a student of Adler's and led one of the guidance centers.

Adler saw human behavior as movement toward or striving toward a sense of belonging (connection) and significance and from a sense of "less than" to a sense of wholeness. He argued that most misbehaviors were really solutions to a different problem (usually a sense of being less than) and that understanding the problem would offer insight into helping the person find more effective and socially useful solutions. He understood that growing and learning as a human being requires the courage to be imperfect. A deep believer in respect and dignity for all, Adler spent a significant amount of his professional time working with people who were part of Vienna's "underclass" and was an advocate for safe working conditions.

Adler observed that we have a deep longing to be part of a community and learning the skills to contribute to the community, to have "social interest," is an important component of long-term mental health. Though he developed his philosophy almost a century ago without the aid of modern technology, current brain science supports his theories, which were based on his careful observation of human behavior.

Why the theory is important:

One of the strengths of Positive Discipline is its strong theoretical framework. As a practitioner one doesn't need to remember a long set of tools or rules about what behaviors might be acceptable or whether a response to an inappropriate behavior is "right." Instead, by returning to theory and asking a few simple questions, one can decide for oneself.

- Is it respectful to the other person? Was it respectful to me?
- Did it lead to a better sense of connection?
- Did it invite the student to have a sense of value, meaning or a sense of "I am capable?"
- Was it encouraging? Did it help bring out the other person's best self?
- Will it be helpful long-term?
- Does it invite a sense of social interest and community? Does it work toward the common good?

Five Criteria for Effective Discipline

Effective Discipline:

1. Helps children feel a sense of connection. (Belonging and significance.)
2. Is mutually respectful and encouraging. (Kind and firm at the same time.)
3. Is effective long - term. (Considers what the child is thinking, feeling, learning, and deciding about himself and his world and what to do in the future to survive or to thrive.)
4. Teaches important social and life skills. (Respect, concern for others, problem solving, and cooperation as well as the skills to contribute to the home, school or larger community.)
5. Invites children to discover how capable they are. (Encourages the constructive use of personal power and autonomy.)

Source: Jane Nelsen, www.positivediscipline.com

In addition to the work of Adler, Positive Discipline has been shaped by the work of Jane Nelsen and Lynn Lott. Several of their significant contributions include:

- The recognition that human beings learn new patterns of behavior best through playing with the material and discovering meaning through experience and contrast instead of by just reading or thinking.
- Moving beyond logical consequences to solutions, which are reasonable, related, respectful and helpful.
- An enormous generosity of spirit which has empowered hundreds of passionate men and women to be able to take this work to their own communities around the world with the expectation that their work is honored and done well, but without expecting to be paid every time it is used.

And finally, this work has been shaped by many students of Jane and Lynn who, while remaining true to Adlerian principles and the experiential nature of the work have drawn the links to brain science, adapted it to their own culture and language and have added their creative ideas. As a result the community and work continues to grow and expand the tools and practices that we all need to invite more respect and peace in the world.

In this section you will find:

- The schematic diagram of the House of Positive Discipline in the Classroom which offers a visual framing of the skills and practices used in schools.
- A one page summary of Adlerian theory as well as a chart comparing Adlerian practices with common school practices.
- Information on Top Card which is a simple and practical version of the elegant concept of Lifestyle developed by Alfred Adler.
- Two versions of the Mistaken Goal Chart, a useful tool for understanding the belief behind the behavior which in turn leads to effective problem solving.
- A short piece on the implications of trauma and attachment on behavior
- A summary of the "brain in the palm of the hand." (Daniel Siegel)

Moving it forward:

If learning about Positive Discipline in the School and Classroom has left you yearning for a deeper understanding of theory:

- Utilize some of the many resources at the end of this manual.
- Join the Positive Discipline community by becoming a member at PositiveDiscipline.org and/or by visiting PositiveDiscipline.ning.com
- The North American Society for Adlerian Society has an annual conference with a track for educators (www.AlfredAdler.org) and there is also a two week international summer conference, ICASSI, sponsored by the Rudolf Dreikurs Summer Institute (www.icassi.net).

House of Positive Discipline in the Classroom

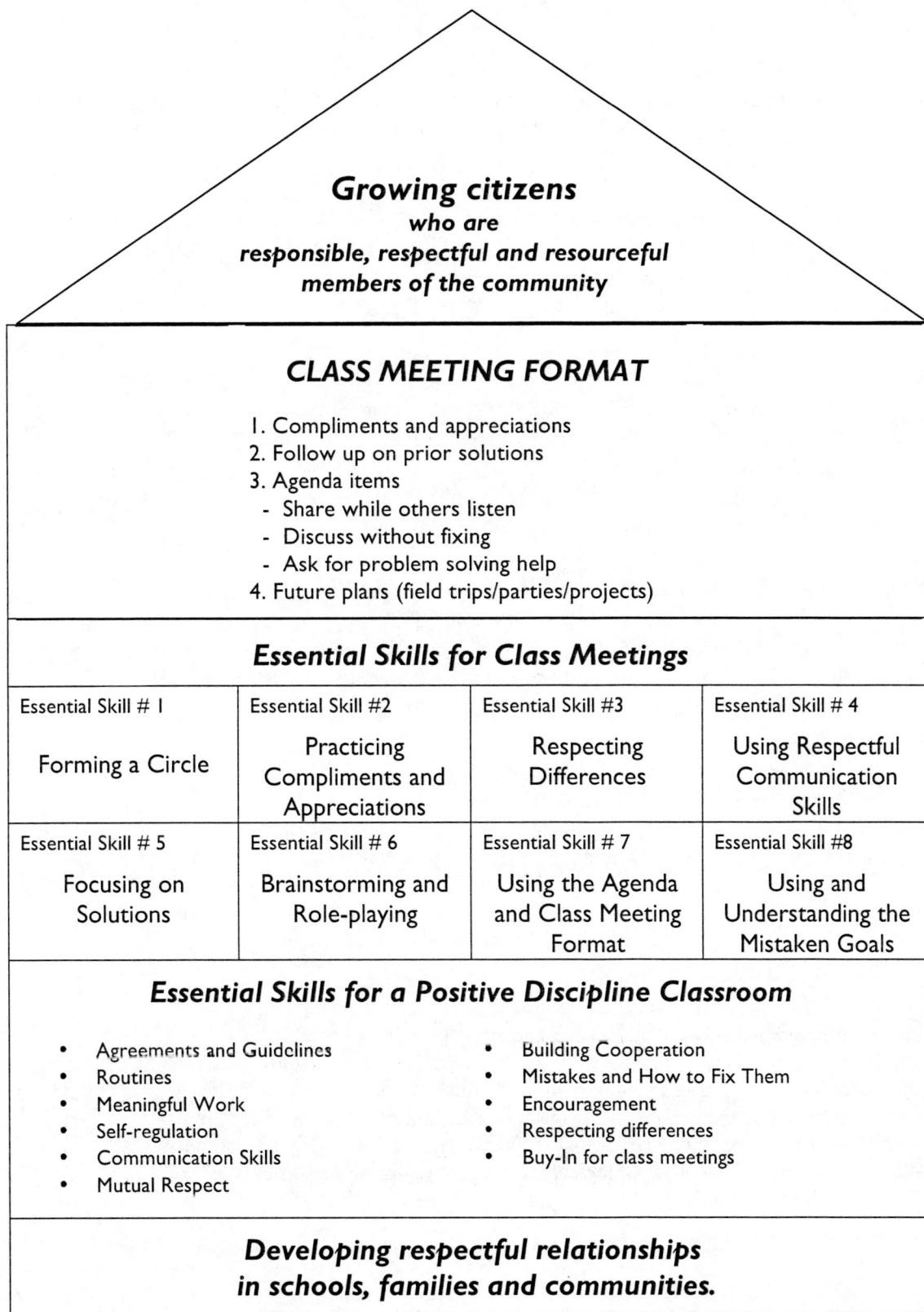

Growing citizens
who are
responsible, respectful and resourceful
members of the community

CLASS MEETING FORMAT

1. Compliments and appreciations
2. Follow up on prior solutions
3. Agenda items
   - Share while others listen
   - Discuss without fixing
   - Ask for problem solving help
4. Future plans (field trips/parties/projects)

Essential Skills for Class Meetings

Essential Skill # 1	Essential Skill #2	Essential Skill #3	Essential Skill # 4
Forming a Circle	Practicing Compliments and Appreciations	Respecting Differences	Using Respectful Communication Skills
Essential Skill # 5	**Essential Skill # 6**	**Essential Skill # 7**	**Essential Skill #8**
Focusing on Solutions	Brainstorming and Role-playing	Using the Agenda and Class Meeting Format	Using and Understanding the Mistaken Goals

Essential Skills for a Positive Discipline Classroom

- Agreements and Guidelines
- Routines
- Meaningful Work
- Self-regulation
- Communication Skills
- Mutual Respect
- Building Cooperation
- Mistakes and How to Fix Them
- Encouragement
- Respecting differences
- Buy-In for class meetings

Developing respectful relationships
in schools, families and communities.

BUILDING THE HOUSE

LAYING THE FOUNDATION

PREPARING THE GROUND

VISION

Adapted from design by Debbie Owen-Sohocki

A Brief Introduction to the Thought of Alfred Adler

Terry Chadsey

Core ideas

1. Behavior is purposive
2. The goal of behavior is belonging (sense of connection) and meaning (significance). Mis-behavior is from a "mis"-taken belief about how to find belonging/meaning.
3. People are continually making decisions based on how their world is perceived.

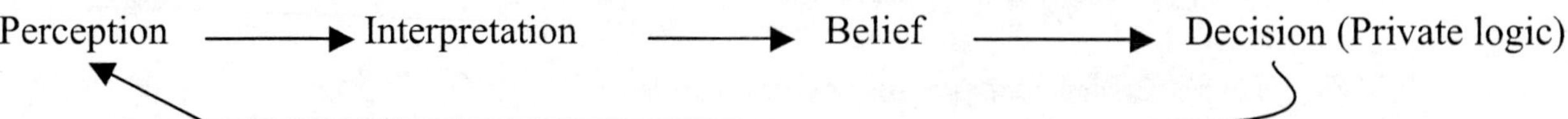

4. Horizontal relationships: Everyone is worthy of equal dignity and respect.

Implications

1. The "problem" is really a "solution" to another problem that is unstated or out of awareness. The mis-behaving child is a discouraged child.
2. Gemeinshaftsgefuehl (Community feeling)
   Being part of a community (belonging/connection)
   Being able to make a contribution to the community (significance/purpose)

Basic tools and principles that flow from Adler's thought

1. Teach life skills
2. Pay attention to the power of perception
3. Focus on encouragement (Connection and presence, not rah-rah)
4. Hold the tension of kindness AND firmness at the same time
5. Look to mutual respect
   Respect for yourself and the situation (firmness)
   Respect for the needs of the child and others (kindness)
6. Assume mistakes to be opportunities to learn.
7. Look to solutions rather than punishment

Five Criteria for Effective Discipline

Effective Discipline:

1. Helps children feel a sense of connection. (Belonging and significance.)
2. Is mutually respectful and encouraging. (Kind and firm at the same time.)
3. Is effective long - term. (Considers what the child is thinking, feeling, learning, and deciding about himself and his world – and what to do in the future to survive or to thrive.)
4. Teaches important social and life skills. (Respect, concern for others, problem solving, and cooperation as well as the skills to contribute to the home, school or larger community.)
5. Invites children to discover how capable they are. (Encourages the constructive use of personal power and autonomy.)

Source: Jane Nelsen, www.positivediscipline.com

Developing Relationships with Children According to the **Dimensions of Kindness and Firmness**

Terry Chadsey

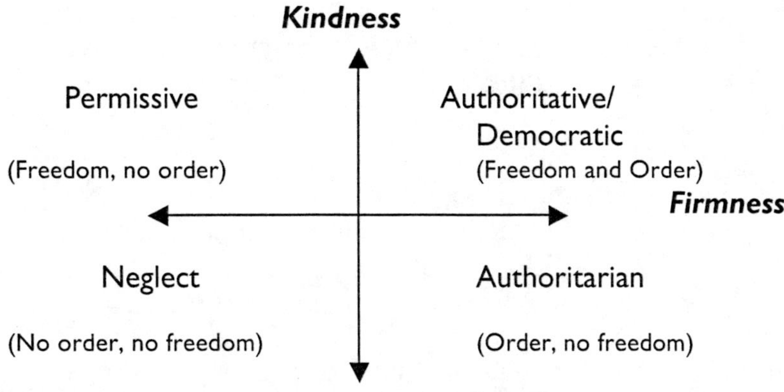

Two Opposing Schools of Thought on Human Behavior

Chart by Terry Chadsey and Jody McVittie

	Dominant and Traditional Practice in American Schools	**The Democratic (Solution Focused) Approach**
Theory based on:	Common practice, Pavlov, Thorndike, Skinner.	Adler, Dreikurs, Dewey, Glasser, Nelsen, Lott, Dinkmeyer, Albert.
Behavior is motivated by:	People respond to rewards and punishments in their environment.	People seek a sense of belonging (connection) and significance (meaning) in their social context.
We have most influence on the behavior of others:	At the moment of response to a specific behavior.	In an ongoing relationship founded on mutual respect.
The most powerful tools for adults are:	Control, rewards, and punishments.	Empathy, understanding the perspective of the student, encouragement, collaborative problem solving, kind AND firm follow through.
"Respect" is:	Obedience and compliance in relationships in which dignity and respect of the adult is primary.	Mutual, in relationships in which each person is equally worthy of dignity and respect.
"Appropriate" response to inappropriate behavior:	Censure, isolation, punishment	Naming without shaming and blaming, identifying the belief behind the behavior, focus on solutions, follow through.
"Appropriate" response to dangerous and destructive behavior:	Censure, isolation, punishment.	Maintaining safety for all, holding the student accountable for their action, followed, at a later time, by solution focused planning and clear follow through.
Student learning is maximized when:	The adult has effective control over student behavior.	The student feels belonging and significance in the classroom.

Discipline: The Development of Self-Control

Laurie Prusso Hatch

The Teacher's Role

It is the role of the teacher to teach children skills and provide them with many opportunities to practice and master the skills that they will need to become successful; this includes the skills of self-control.

Your beliefs influence your thoughts and feelings…
Your thoughts and feelings influence your decisions…
Your decisions determine your actions…
What you do has a direct effect on a student!

Which student do you know?

Trouble Maker	Inquisitive and curious
Disrespectful	Outspoken
Boastful	Confident
Destructive	Creative
Hyperactive	Energetic
Bossy	Leader
Rebellious	Independent
Stubborn	Persistent
Non-compliant	Self-directed
Picky	Sensitive
Defiant	Decisive

Seeing a student through the lens of his or her strengths

- Is encouraging to the student,
- Invites behavior that is more helpful than hurtful,
- Helps students redirect their behavior to become more socially useful,
- Makes it easier for the educator to work with the student to solve problems more effectively.

**When people face challenges in a supportive environment, growth occurs.
When people face challenges in a non-supportive environment, avoidance occurs.
The teacher's role is to encourage growth.**

"We must realize that we *cannot build on deficiencies, only on strength.* We cannot help our children – or anyone else – to have faith in themselves as long as we have no faith in them."

Dreikurs *Social Equality: The Challenge of Today*, p. 122 (emphasis in original)

The Scaffolded Approach to Discipline

From Preventing School Violence by Sugai, Horner & Walker, adapted by Jody McVittie

Solution-focused discipline speaks the same language as RTI (Response to Intervention) and MTSS (Multi- Tiered System of Support)

School-wide discipline must address three levels of need

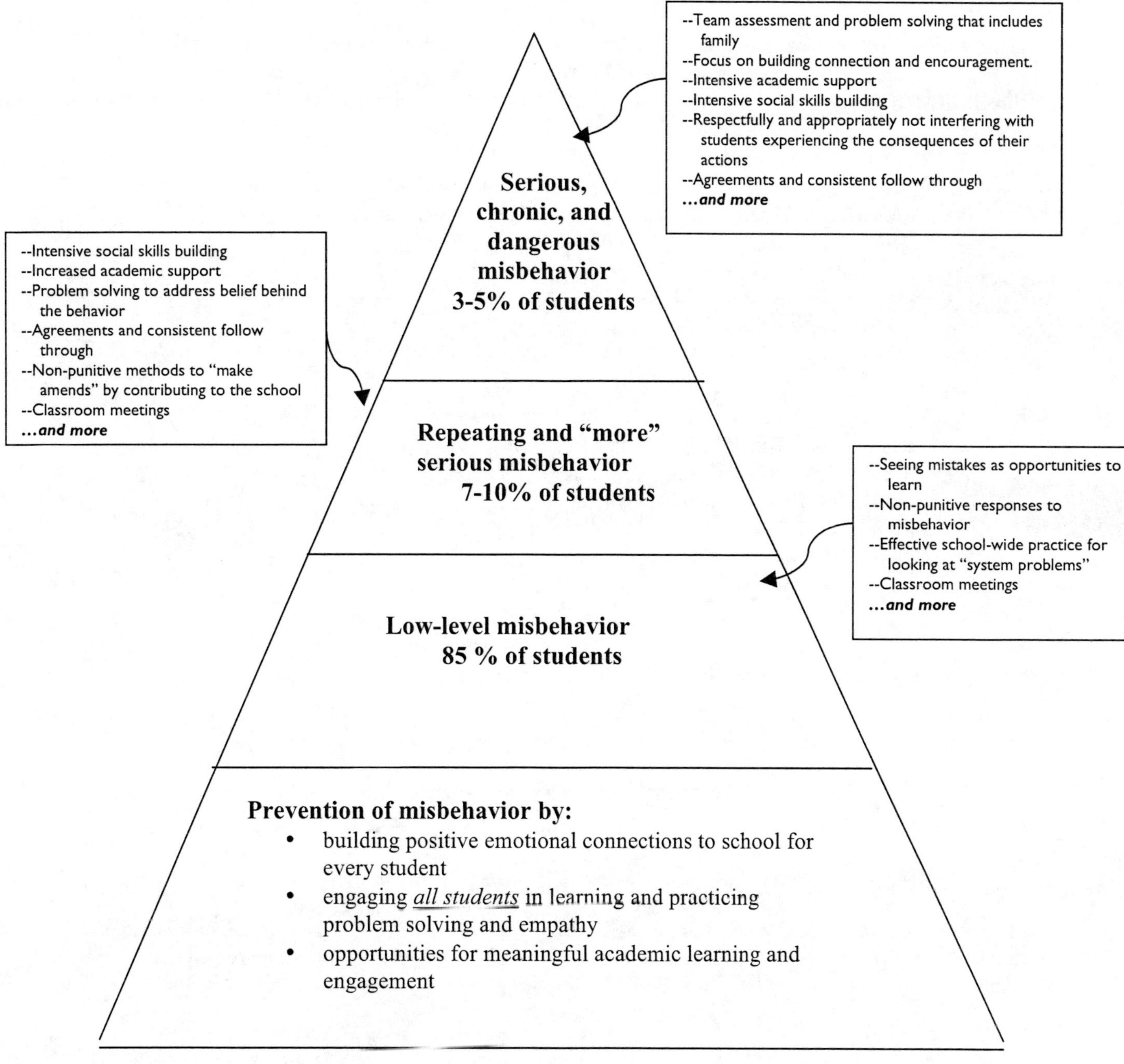

--Team assessment and problem solving that includes family
--Focus on building connection and encouragement.
--Intensive academic support
--Intensive social skills building
--Respectfully and appropriately not interfering with students experiencing the consequences of their actions
--Agreements and consistent follow through
...and more
Serious, chronic, and dangerous misbehavior
3-5% of students
--Intensive social skills building
--Increased academic support
--Problem solving to address belief behind the behavior
--Agreements and consistent follow through
--Non-punitive methods to "make amends" by contributing to the school
--Classroom meetings
...and more
Repeating and "more" serious misbehavior
7-10% of students
--Seeing mistakes as opportunities to learn
--Non-punitive responses to misbehavior
--Effective school-wide practice for looking at "system problems"
--Classroom meetings
...and more
Low-level misbehavior
85 % of students
Prevention of misbehavior by:
building positive emotional connections to school for every student
engaging all students in learning and practicing problem solving and empathy
opportunities for meaningful academic learning and engagement

Respect throughout:

Respect for self: *What do I need?*

Respect for others: *What does this student need? What do other students need?*

Respect for the situation: *What does the situation demand?*

Some Core Positive Discipline Concepts

Courage (from the root word *cor* – Latin, heart) is the small step you take towards being more of who you truly are, when it might be easier to take a step in another direction.. So when you *encourage* someone, you are creating a space for him or her to take that step toward his or her best self.

The Courage to be Imperfect:
What is a mistake? What makes it a big mistake, or a small mistake? Children sometimes "learn" that they "are" a mistake and feel shame, instead of understanding that everyone "makes" mistakes.
How is life different when we really understand that mistakes are opportunities to learn? Who would you be without all of the mistakes you have learned from?

Recovery From a Mistake *(Repair is critical!)* (adapted from Jane Nelsen, *Positive Discipline*):
- Re-gather: Self-calm and find your rational self before starting the "repair"
- Recognize: *"Whoops, I made a mistake."*
- Reconcile: *"I'm sorry."*
- Resolve (Re-Solve): *"How can we work on this together to make it better?" (or some variation of this idea)*

Results of Punishment (from Jane Nelsen, *Positive Discipline*)
- Resentment: "This is unfair. I can't trust adults."
- Revenge: "They are winning now, but I'll get even."
- Rebellion: "I'll do just the opposite to prove I don't have to do it their way."
- Retreat:
  from others :"I won't get caught next time."
  or from one's self: "I'm a bad person."

Solutions: Reasonable, Respectful, Related AND Helpful

"A misbehaving child is a discouraged child."

Rudolf Dreikurs

"The essentials for living in a democratic society can be simply stated...*The principle implies mutual respect, respect for the dignity of others and respect for oneself.* The principle is expressed in a combination of firmness and kindness. Firmness implies self-respect; kindness, respect for the others."

- Dreikurs, *Social Equality: The Challenge of Today* Emphasis in original

The Jumbled School House

The jumbled schoolhouse analogy is a powerful visual tool to help schools recognize the importance of taking a whole-school mission driven approach to improving services and outcomes for students. Initially developed by Dr. Maurice Elias and the Developing Safe and Civil Schools (DSACS) team[5], the metaphor helps educators understand that without a guiding framework, even the best intended practices can lead to fragmentation. Dr. Elias and his team of researchers assert that an effective social-emotional/character development framework is the essential piece that links the academic program, parent and community involvement, and all systems and programs within the school building. The resulting synergy helps ensure students receive the skills they need for success in life.

The activity, "The Jumbled School House," presented in this manual utilizes the diagram below. Permission to print, enlarge, or convert the image below to PowerPoint is granted from Dr. Elias for use with this activity. When presenting the activity credit should clearly be given to Dr. Elias and the DSACS Team. The authors of the *PDSC Leaders' Guide* and the PDA are appreciative of Dr. Elias' generosity in granting this permission.

If you would like to read further, explore the site: The Collaborative for Academic, Social and Emotional Learning (CASEL) www.casel.org

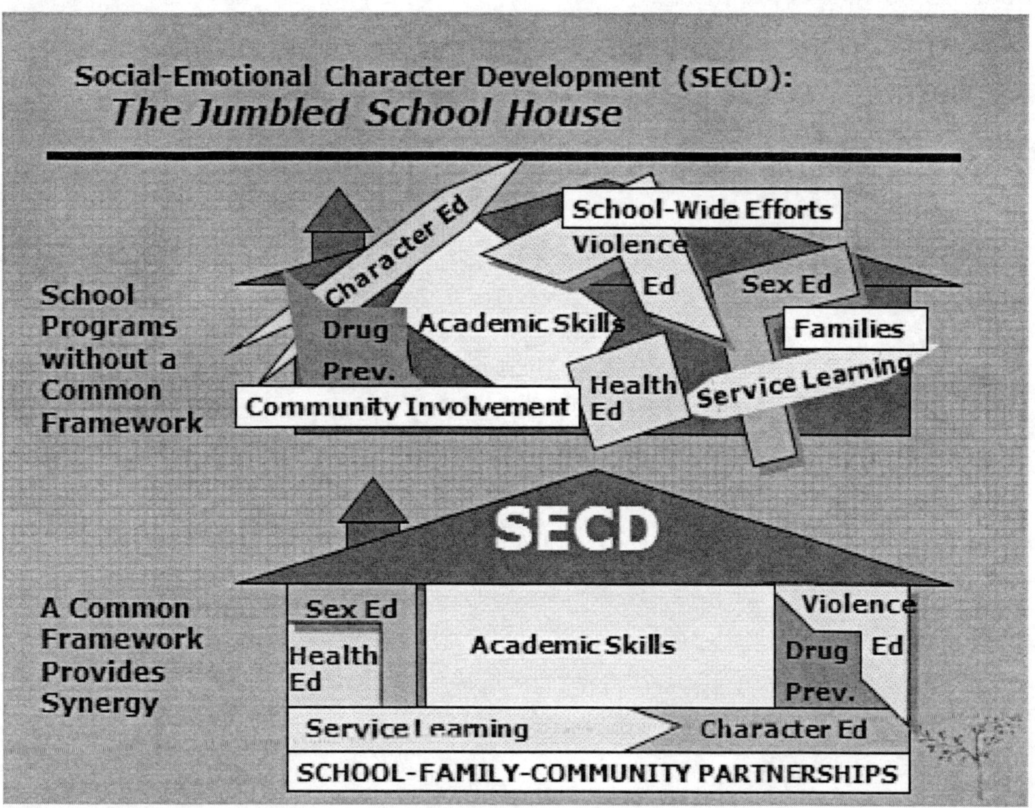

- Enlarged and cut-out pieces of Jumbled Schoolhouse are available at www.positivediscipline.org. Go to Jumbled School House under Free Resources and Links to retrieve copy or the power point version of the jumbled schoolhouse.

---

5 Elias, Maurice J. and the DSACS_SECD Team (www.teachSECD.com). Guidelines for putting the pieces together: How to go from the jumbled schoolhouse to the synergized schoolhouse. Retrieved from www.docstoc.com/docs/91651933

My Top Card Handout

Jane Nelsen

Rejection and Hassles	Criticism and Ridicule	Stress and Pain	Meaninglessness and Unimportance

1. Label your least favorite box #1. Label your second least favorite box #2.

2. My top card is ___________________ (the box ranked No. 1)

3. My style is ______________________ (the box ranked No. 2)

4. A bumper sticker for my top card could be:

____

5. My best assets are:

____

____

____

____

6. My liabilities are:

____

____

____

____

7. My top card may invite from others:

____

____

____

8. Specific steps for improvement:

____

____

____

Teaching Ups and Downs and Possibilities of Top Cards

Lynn Lott

Top Card	Possible Teaching Assets	Possible Teaching Liabilities	May Need to Practice
CONTROL (Eagle)	May teach children: Organizational skills Leadership skills Productive persistence Assertiveness Respect for law and order	Rigid Controlling May invite rebellion and resistance or unhealthy pleasing.	Letting go Offering choices Asking what and how questions Involving children in decisions Class meetings
PLEASING (Chameleon)	May help children learn to be friendly, considerate and non-aggressive. Peacemakers, compromisers, volunteers, and champions of the underdog.	Doormats, keep score ("now you owe me"). May invite resentment, depression, or revenge.	Have faith in children to solve their own problems Joint problem solving Emotional honesty Class meetings
COMFORT (Turtle)	Model for children benefits of being easygoing, diplomatic, predictable, and to enjoy simple pleasures.	Permissiveness, which may invite children to be spoiled and demanding. More interest in com-fort than in the "needs of the situation."	Creating routines Setting goals Solving problems together Teaching life skills Allowing children to experience consequences of their choices Class meetings
SUPERIORITY (Lion)	Model success and achievement. Teach children to assess quality and motivate to excellence.	Lecture, preach, expect too much. Invite feelings of inadequacy and failure to "measure up." See things in terms of right and wrong instead of possibilities.	Letting go of need to be right Getting into child's world and supporting needs and goals Unconditional love Enjoying the process and developing a sense of humor Holding class meetings where all ideas are valued.

Mistaken Goal Chart

Jane Nelsen and Lynn Lott, www.positivediscipline.com

The Child's goal is:	If the parent/ teacher feels:	And tends to react by:	And if the child's response is:	The belief behind the child's behavior is:	Coded messages	Parent/teacher proactive and **encouraging** responses include:
Undue Attention (to keep others busy or to get special service)	Annoyed Irritated Worried Guilty	Reminding. Coaxing. Doing things for the child he/she could do for him/herself.	Stops temporarily, but later resumes same or another disturbing behavior	I count (belong) only when I'm being noticed or getting special service. I'm only important when I'm keeping you busy with me.	**Notice Me. Involve Me Usefully.**	Redirect by involving child in a useful task to gain attention. Say what you will do. (Example: I love you and will spend time with you later.") Avoid special service. Have faith in child to deal with feelings (don't fix or rescue). Plan regular special time. Help child create routine charts. Engage child in problem solving. Use family/class meetings. Set up nonverbal signals. Ignore behavior with hand on shoulder.
Misguided Power (to be boss)	Angry Challenged Threatened Defeated	Fighting. Giving in. Thinking, *"You can't get away with it* or *I'll make you."* Wanting to be right.	Intensifies behavior. Complies with defiance. Feels he/she's won when parent/teacher is upset even if he/she has to comply. Passive power (says *yes* but doesn't follow through).	I belong only when I'm boss, in control, or proving no one can boss me. You can't make me.	**Let Me Help. Give Me Choices.**	Redirect to positive power by asking for help. Offer limited choices. Don't fight and don't give in. Withdraw from conflict. Be firm and kind. Don't talk—act. Decide what you will do. Let routines be the boss. Leave and calm down. Develop mutual respect. Set a few reasonable limits. Practice follow-through. Use family/class meetings.
Revenge (to get even)	Hurt Disappointed Disbelieving Disgusted	Hurting back. Shaming. Thinking, *"How could you do such a thing?"*	Retaliates. Intensifies. Escalates the same behavior or chooses another weapon.	I don't think I belong so I'll hurt others as I feel hurt. I can't be liked or loved.	**I'm Hurting. Validate My Feelings.**	Acknowledge hurt feelings. Avoid feeling hurt. Avoid punishment and retaliation. Build trust. Use reflective listening. Share your feelings. Make amends. Show you care. Encourage strengths. Don't take sides. Use family/class meetings.
Assumed Inadequacy (to give up and be left alone)	Despair Hopeless Helpless Inadequate	Giving up. Doing things for the child that he/she could do for him/herself. Over-helping.	Retreats further. Becomes passive. Shows no improvement. Is not responsive.	I can't belong because I'm not perfect, so I'll convince others not to expect any-thing of me. I am helpless and unable. It's no use trying because I won't do it right.	**Don't Give Up On Me. Show Me A Small Step.**	Break task down into small steps. Stop all criticism. Encourage any positive attempt. Have faith in child's abilities. Focus on assets. Don't pity. Don't give up. Set up opportunities for success. Teach skills—show how, but don't do for. Enjoy the child. Build on his/her interests. Use family/class meetings.

The Belief Behind the Behavior – A key for mistaken beliefs.

Based on the Psychology of Alfred Adler and Rudolf Dreikurs, adapted by Jody McVittie from similar schema by Steven Maybell and Jane Nelsen. 3/06

1. Student's Behavior	*2. Adult's feeling*	3. Adult's mistaken reactions	4. Student's response	***5. The student's belief***	6. Effective prevention (Encouragement)	7. Effective responses (More encouragement)	8. Goal
Nuisance Show-off Clown Disruptive Pesters Blurting out Teacher's pet	•*Annoyed* •*Irritated*	Reminding Coaxing	Stops temporarily, but later resumes same or another disturbing behavior	***I count or belong only when I am getting attention, when others notice me.***	Spend special time Provide opportunities to contribute. Teach connection skills Set up routines Class meetings	Hear: "Notice me, involve me." "I care about you and. . ." ______ (Example: I care about you and will spend time with you later.") Redirect by assigning a task so student can gain useful attention Use problem-solving Touch without words Set up nonverbal signals	Undue Attention
Acts pitiful Acts helpless Acts scared Acts whiny Demanding	•*Worried* •*Guilt* •*Sorry for* •*Responsible for*	Reminding Taking Responsibility Making excuses for the student Doing things for the student he/she could do for him/herself	Acts incapable or even more demanding often with engaging drama	***I count or belong only when I'm keeping others busy with me.*** ***I am special.*** ***I'm not sure I can do it for myself, "Do it for me."***	Make room for learning from mistakes. Become "incompetent" Avoid special service or pampering Provide opportunities to contribute Class meetings	Set up routines Use problem solving. Take time for training Allow disappointment and frustration as new skills are learned. Promote autonomy Practice self respect	Special Service
Defiant Argumentative Passive - aggressive Apathetic Takes over leadership of any group	•*Challenged* •*Defeated* •*Provoked* -*Indignation* - *(Angry)*	Fighting Forcing Giving in Thinking "You can't get away with it" or "I'll make you" Wanting to be right Wanting to be in charge/control Punishing	Intensifies behavior Defiant - compliance Feels he/she's won when adult is upset. Passive power	***I count or belong only when I'm boss, in control, or proving no one can boss me.*** ***"You can't make me."*** ***"You can't stop me."***	Provide opportunities to contribute in useful ways Set a few reasonable limits (kind and firm) Give choices Develop mutual respect Mutual problem solving. Practice follow through Class meetings	Hear: "Let me help, give me choices" Let routines be the boss Don't fight and don't give in. Withdraw from conflict (leave and calm down) Redirect to positive power by asking for help Be firm and kind Act, don't talk Decide what you will do (vs. what students should do) Use positive time out	Misguided power
Hurtful Vindictive Rude Abusive Self destructive	•*Hurt* •*Disbelieving* •*Spiteful* - *(Angry)*	Retaliating Getting even Punishing Play victim - thinking "How could you do this to me?"	Retaliates Intensifies Escalates the same behavior or chooses another weapon	***I don't think I belong (or count) so I'll hurt others as I feel hurt.*** ***I can't be liked or loved.***	Teach/ use self soothing and calming tools Show you care Build relationship Teach/ use "I" statements Avoid blame or shame Encourage strengths Avoid taking sides Class meetings	Hear: "I'm hurting" Connect: acknowledge feelings Emotional honesty Make amends Teach to make amends Avoid acting on hurt feelings Avoid punishment and retaliation Clear and appropriate follow through	Revenge
Withdrawal Indifferent to work Pessimism Hopelessness	•*Discouraged* •*Futility* - *Helpless (low energy)*	Compare student to others Criticize Doing for the student Giving up	Retreats further Passive No response No improvement	***I can't count or belong because I'm inferior to others.*** ***It's no use trying because if I did others would find out how inferior I am.*** ***I'm not perfect, so I'll convince others not to expect anything of me.***	Give responsibilities Show confidence Show faith Teach routines Teach how to break tasks into smaller pieces Model mistakes: it is okay to be imperfect Class meetings	Hear: "Don't give up on me" Show small steps Remind of past successes and strengths Show faith and confidence Take care of yourself and get support.	Inadequacy or Avoidance of humiliation

Understanding Attachment and the Development of Beliefs

Penny Davis, MA, CPDT, adapted from 'Attachment Parenting' by Grossmont College Foster and Kinship Education

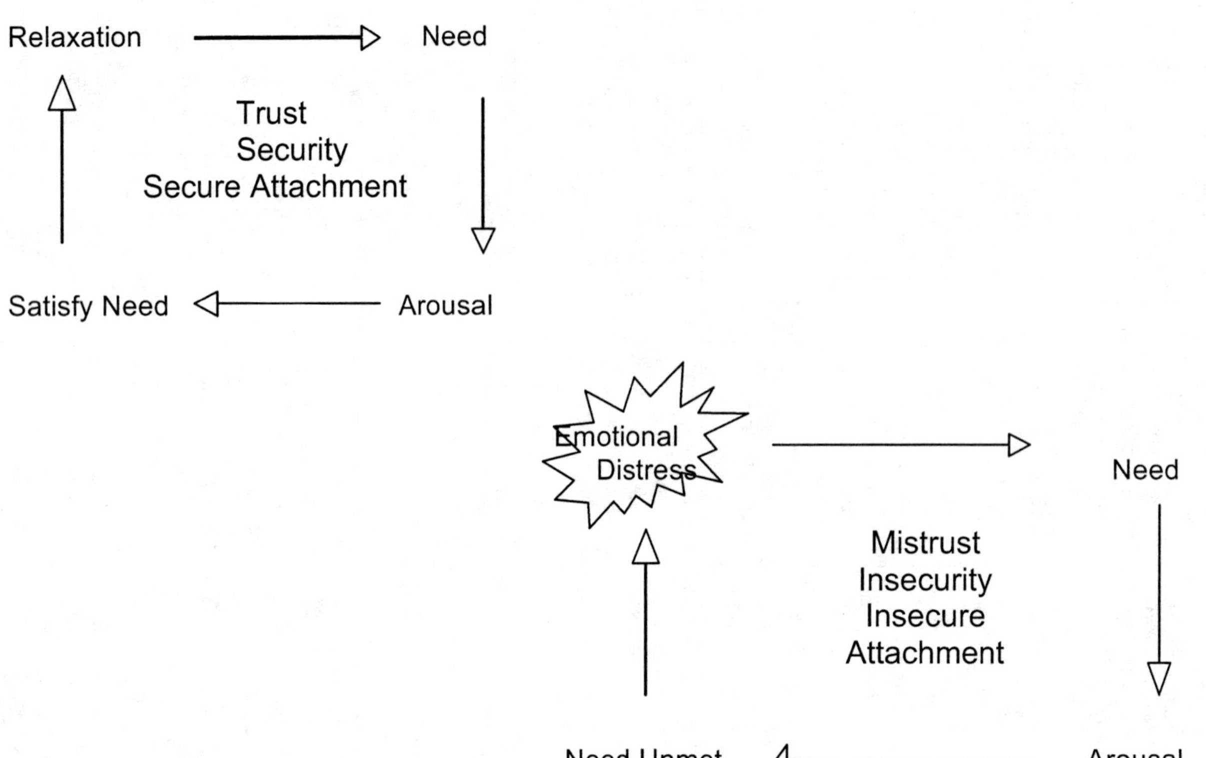

Attachment Building Blocks

Penny Davis, MA, CPDA, adapted from 'Attachment Parenting' by Grossmont College Foster and Kinship Education

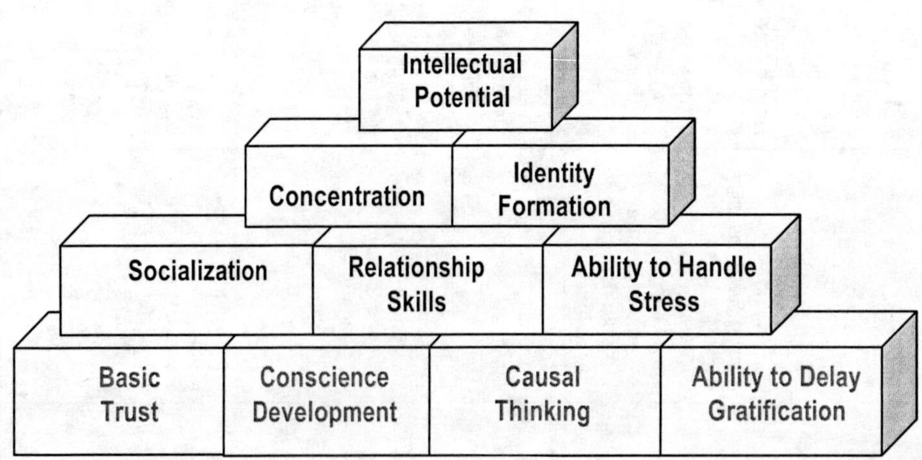

Rebuilding the Foundation for Students with Insecure Attachments or Trauma

Jody McVittie, MD, CPDLT

Basic Trust

Routines (including class meetings)
Consistency and reliability in the relationship.
Relationships based on dignity and respect (firm and kind)
Listening to their story

Causal Thinking

"What" and "how" questions
Limited choices
Focusing on solutions

Conscience Development

"What" and "how" questions
Class meetings
Gradual building of empathy (being listened to, feeling felt)
Respecting differences (Activity: It's A Jungle Out There)

Ability to Delay Gratification

Routines
Consistency
Relationships built on dignity and respect (firm and kind)
Class meetings – working with peers
Mistakes are opportunities to learn

Identity Formation and Intellectual Potential

Classroom jobs and responsibility
Being able to contribute in meaningful ways
Using "I" statements and learning language for emotions
Opportunities to practice during play
Learning how to make amends and fix mistakes instead of "paying for them"
"It seems like you feel..... because..."

Relationship Skills and Socialization

Adult relationships based on dignity and respect (firm and kind)
Class meetings
Problem solving
Wheel of choice
Opportunities for play and practice and making mistakes
Mistakes are opportunities to learn

Ability to Handle Stress, and Concentration

De- escalation tools (modeled, taught, expected)
Teaching students about their own brain (brain in the palm of the hand)
Using "I statements"
Learning language for emotions
Space for "chilling out" (Positive Time Out or Chill Down Time – CDT)
Class meeting to be heard and validated, and to recognize that others have similar feelings.
Mistakes are opportunities to learn

> We learn best from those with whom we are in caring, mutually respectful relationships that promote independence. Such supportive relationships enable students from diverse backgrounds to feel comfortable bringing their personal experiences into the classroom, discover their common humanity and feel as though they are viewed as assets to the school community.
>
> Learning First Alliance Every Child Learning: Safe and Supportive Schools

Working with Students Exposed to Trauma

Jody McVittie

Children exposed to trauma struggle to:

- Accurately perceive safety (over perceive danger).
- Self-regulate (attention, behavior, emotion).
- Hold a self image that includes the belief that they matter.
- Succeed academically and or socially at school.

What trauma can look like in the classroom (and school)

Adapted from: *Helping Traumatized Children Learn*

Students exposed to trauma may:

- Disrupt the ability to process verbal information and use language to communicate. (May make it difficult to follow instructions.)
- Be less skilled in using language to forge social relationships and more skilled using language to build walls between themselves and those perceived to be dangerous or threatening.
- Have limited problem-solving skills.
- Struggle with sequential ordering and therefore not be able to organize (thoughts, feelings, if-then events, multi-step tasks) which in turn results in difficulty reading, writing and with critical thinking. Interfere with a student's understanding of behavior and consequences.
- Not have internalized cause and effect relationships. This means that they cannot easily predict events, sense their power over events or make meaning of "consequences."
- Struggle to see the world from the point of view of another.
- Struggle to focus and attend to what is happening in the classroom because their brains are preoccupied with ensuring safety /warding off danger.
- Struggle to self regulate and recognize emotions. This results in poor impulse control, trouble reading social cues, and lack of a predictable sense of self. (Self regulation is a predictor of academic success).
- Have low executive functions.
- Be slow to trust adults or peers.
- Struggle to engage with academic material effectively.

The Student Intervention Team Meeting

For students who have experienced trauma

Thinking it though:

- How do you establish trust? (Who should be there? Who will be the advocate for the student? What kind of practice is necessary?)
- How do you establish safety? (What are the ground rules? How will the student be supported – ALWAYS?)
- What are the student's strengths?
- What doable piece of the challenge needs to be addressed?
- How can the student use his/her strengths to meet the challenge?
- How do you work with family/care givers to frame things in a helpful way – to invite them to see the student's best side?
- What is a reasonable amount of change to expect?
- What skills will be needed for the student to be successful?
- Who is going to be responsible? And for what?
- What is the follow through going to look like? (Who, when, how, next meeting?)

* * * * *Remember to take care of yourself. Vicarious trauma is real.* * * * *

The Brain in the Palm of your Hand

From *Parenting from the Inside Out*, Daniel Seigel and Mary Hartzell

Your Wrist and Palm: Brain Stem. Responsible for survival instincts: flight, freeze or fight. Autonomic ("automatic") functions.

Your Thumb: Mid-brain. The amygdala (the brain's safety radar), memories, emotions.

Your Fingers over **your Thumb**: Cortex. Perception, motor action, speech, higher processing and what we normally call "thinking."

Your Fingernails: Pre-frontal cortex – a primary integration center for the brain, almost like a "switchboard" that makes sure messages get where they need to go. Documented functions of the pre-frontal cortex are: regulation of body through autonomic nervous system, emotional regulation, regulation of interpersonal relationships, response flexibility, intuition, mindsight, self-awareness, letting go of fears, morality.

What happens when you are stressed, overwhelmed, or trying to deal with traumatic or painful memories? The pre-frontal cortex shuts down; it no longer functions. (This is temporary, thank goodness!) You have "flipped your lid". You can't use most of the 9 functions above--and you can't learn without them. To engage and to learn, you need to calm down and bring the pre-frontal cortex back into functioning. Watch Daniel Siegel explain it: http://www.youtube.com/watch?v=DD-lfP1FBFk

Mirror Neurons: The "monkey see, monkey do" neurons that play a key role in social interaction, connection and learning. Go to: http://www.pbs.org/wgbh/nova/sciencenow/3204/01.html to see an excellent 14-minute Nova episode on **mirror neurons.**

Your brain, when the prefrontal cortex is working:

Integrative functioning (the high road)

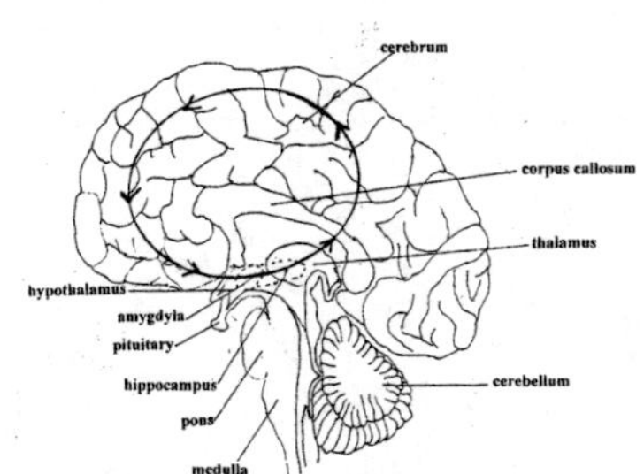

Integrative functioning: "A form of processing information that involves the higher, rational, reflective thought process of the mind. High-road processing allows for mindfulness, flexibility in our responses and an integrating sense of self awareness. The high road involves the prefrontal cortex in its processes." Siegel and Hartzell, *Parenting from the Inside Out.*

Non- integrated function (flipping your lid, the low road)

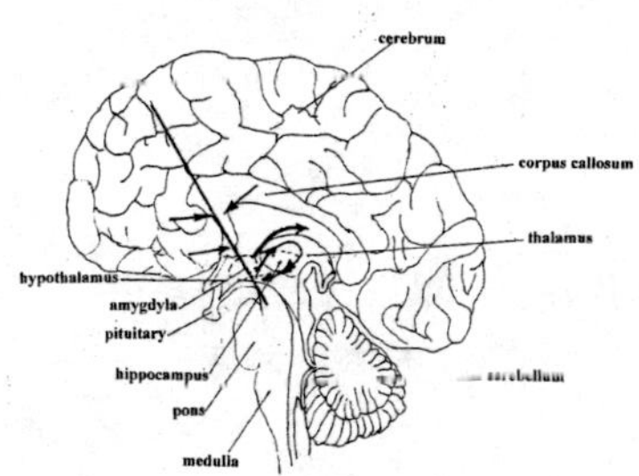

"Low road functioning involves the shutting down of the higher processes of the mind and leaves the individual in a state of intense emotions, impulsive reactions, rigid and repetitive responses and lacking in self reflection and the consideration of another's point of view. Involvement of the prefrontal cortex is shut off when one is on the low road." Siegel and Hartzell, *Parenting from the Inside Out.*

Drawings adapted from Siegel and Hartzell, Parenting from the Inside Out. P. 157

In a sense, misbehavior is a shout into echo canyon; the echo (our response) is more important than the shout. If we build our students' self-confidence and give them recognition for useful, constructive behavior, they won't need to shout.

- Dinkmeyer et al.,*STET: Systematic Training for Effective Teaching*, P. 9

Class Meetings

A quick summary:
A Positive Discipline class meeting is a regular, 15 to 20 minute gathering in a circle that follows a very specific format and uses an agenda. Class meetings use an object chosen by the class as a talking stick and begin with compliments. After compliments, previous solutions are reviewed and new problems that have been written on the agenda are addressed by the class. Classrooms that are skilled have student led meetings.

Why class meetings are important:
Class meetings offer the opportunity for students to practice the skills they are learning using real-time, relevant problems. In the process they also learn many skills that foster academic success including:

- Using their voice
- Listening to others
- The practice of looking at issues from different perspectives
- Seeing mistakes as an opportunity to learn
- Seeing the strengths of their peers
- Understanding of the power of collaboration
- A sense of socially useful influence and capability
- The sense of accomplishment that comes from contributing usefully.

In this section you will find:
Two brief guides for class meetings. The activities used to teach class meetings are in *Positive Discipline in the School and Classroom Teachers' Guide: Activities for Students.*

Moving it forward:
Though there are other resources for reading about class meetings, our sense is that the best way to learn about the power of class meetings is to experience them. We work with teachers regularly who talk about what they have learned from their students and the class meeting process.

- Use *Positive Discipline in the School and Classroom Teachers' Guide: Activities for Students.* Teach your students the Preparing the Ground Skills and the Essential Skills for Class Meetings.
- As your students become more skilled challenge your class to extend their reach a bit more broadly. What can be done to improve the school? The community? How else might they contribute?

A class meeting story:
Early in the spring, students in a Seattle 5th-grade class started bringing some silly putty to school and used it to occupy their hands instead of fidgeting. One week later, the silly putty became a bit of a problem and some of the silly putty (being used inappropriately) got put in time out on a shelf. And then it disappeared. This was stressful for Liz (not her real name) as she had saved her money to buy the silly putty.

At their class meeting, the students talked about how embarrassing it would be to admit that you had taken the silly putty. They talked about mistakes being opportunities to learn and that no one would be punished. Nothing happened. Then Clyde (not his real name), prime suspect #1, "found" the silly putty in a cupboard – but denied having taken it. The class was suspicious but the teacher set very clear expectations that no one would be blamed without evidence. The next morning, shortly before their scheduled class meeting students were working in small groups Clyde blurted out, "Alright, I did it!" Not everyone heard this but Liz did. She asked to meet with Clyde and the two of them found a quiet place to talk.

The teacher had some concerns. He knew that Clyde's name was on the agenda for another problem. He didn't know whether Clyde would be willing to come to the class meeting after his confession and didn't think that it would be a good idea to tackle the next problem when Clyde was feeling vulnerable. He decided to have the class meeting but only do compliments.

Liz and Clyde arrived just as the class meeting started and found places to sit in the circle. The student leader started the meeting and announced that compliments would be given as "give or get." Clyde was sitting three spaces away from the leader, curled over himself. He sat up when he got the talking stick and complimented Liz for being a friend and listening to him. Liz was about 4 students later and complimented Clyde for being a good friend and listening to her. Two students later James (who had put Clyde on the agenda for the other problem) complimented Clyde for being a good friend. Then another student and another complimented Clyde. One compliment was "I compliment you for being a friend and I trust you." Clyde began to uncurl his body and a tear ran down his right cheek. Several students asked for a compliment and picked the student to give a compliment. Clyde began to partly raise his hand to volunteer to give a compliment. He was invited to give the next compliment. This was followed with more compliments for Clyde. The last one was from a boy who said, "I compliment you for being open with your emotions, the happy ones and the unhappy ones.

No adult prompted or commented on the abundance of compliments for Clyde. It just happened. To conclude the meeting the teacher reminded the students that as a class, over the year they had had several struggles and each time they had been up to the challenge – and that he felt that they had once again met a significant challenge successfully. He told them that the problem solving would happen at the next meeting and they ended with a brief fun rhythm activity.

After the meeting, one of the students remarked under his breath after the circle, "Clyde got nine compliments!" (From a class of 28.)

The teacher saw this meeting as a watershed meeting for his class; partly because of how they welcomed Clyde back in, partly because James initiated the repetitive compliments – James who had been struggling with Clyde all year. He recognized the courage modeled by Clyde and Liz. The teacher also understood that if he had not "prepared the ground" by teaching about mistakes, about differences, compliments, and encouragement, these students would not have had the skills they needed to come together, forgive and welcome Clyde back into their community.

The Class Meeting

Lynn Lott

Purpose of the Class Meeting

1. Skill building

a. The courage to think
b. How to think
c. Problem solving
d. Mutual respect
e. Communication skills
    1. Listening
    2. Expressing thoughts and feelings
    3. Respecting differences
f. Useful power
g. Practice in planning events

2. Self Reliance

a. Self-confidence based on skills
b. Self-esteem based on a sense of belonging
c. Courage based on the ability to make a difference

3. Problem solving

a. Ownership through participation
b. Social interest
c. Practice in helping each other
d. Discipline problems decrease when kids are involved

SIX CRITERIA FOR SUCCESSFUL CLASS MEETINGS

1. Have them regularly (3-5 times per week for elementary school)
2. Form a circle
3. Focus on solutions
4. Pass an item to speak
5. Allow student who put problem on agenda (or student who is focus of the problem) to choose a helpful solution
6. Allow time for all to learn the process.

Adult attitudes and skills necessary to accomplish the above:

1. A sincere desire to create an atmosphere of mutual respect for students and adults at all times.
2. Faith in the abilities of young people to use wisdom and learn skills. (Act like a broken record.)
3. An interest in long-range results for young people rather than short-range. (Replace authoritarian methods with democratic methods.)
4. Replacing lectures with questioning skills that draw forth the wisdom of young people. (*Ask*, "What?" instead of *telling* what.)
5. An interest in knowing what students think. (Getting into their world.)
6. Giving choices rather than issuing edicts.
7. Eliminate punishment and reward in favor of problem-solving, discussion, sharing and sometimes natural or logical consequences.
8. Winning cooperation instead of using control.
9. Patience. The process takes time.

Class Meetings: A Brief Summary for Teachers

Suzanne Smitha

Purpose	1. To give compliments 3. To solve problems. 2. To help each other 4. To plan events (From an adult's perspective, the main purpose is to teach and practice life skills.)
Schedule	At least 3 times per week. Hold firm to a maximum of 20 minutes per meeting.
Arrangement	Everyone (including teacher) in a circle, seated at the same level.
Guidelines	Set by the group. Key: Helpful not Hurtful
Compliments	"_________, I would like to compliment you for _____." Receiver responds, "Thank you." *Use an object* to pass around the circle to indicate who speaks. It is *always okay* to pass (to choose not to speak). Compliments focus on helpfulness and accomplishments.
Agenda	Use a chart, box or notebook. Agree on process for putting items on the agenda.
Problems	Only address items placed on the agenda in advance. (Cool-off time is important) Problems get solved one by one, in order received. Incomplete agenda items get carried from one meeting to the next. The person with the problem chooses how to address it at the meeting: • Share feelings, or • Discuss without fixing, or • Ask for problem-solving help Suggestions are reasonable, related, respectful and helpful. Role-plays are used when helpful for the problems and /or solutions. Choosing solutions: • Whole group problems: class votes. • Student-to-student problems: students involved choose solution that works for both students. Note taking: • Scribe writes down all of the suggestions and marks which solution was chosen. • This is kept as part of the class meeting record.
Planning	Free time, field trips, appropriate academic content, due dates, etc.
Roles	Leader, Scribe, and when more skilled, a "Helpful not Hurtful Monitor" (see *Teachers' Guide*, referenced below). Rotate roles periodically.
Parents	Communicate process and skill development gained from class meetings.
References	*Positive Discipline in the School and Classroom Teachers' Guide, Activities for Students*, by LaSala, McVittie & Smitha *Positive Discipline in the Classroom,* 4th Ed., Nelsen, Lott and Glenn (Both available at www.positivediscipline.com)

Teacher Helping Teacher Problem-Solving Steps

Lynn Lott and Jane Nelsen

A quick summary:

The Teachers Helping Teachers Problem-Solving Steps process is an effective and powerful practice that allows teachers to work with peers to solve nagging classroom problems. Teachers "grow their toolbox" for effective responses and often feel encouraged and empowered by the process. In our experience, teachers using these steps as a team quickly improve their skills using the Mistaken Goal Chart and gain helpful insight into the world of their students. The process eliminates the endless analysis and the search for causes that lead to blame and excuses without helpful action.

Why the Teachers Helping Teachers Problem Solving Steps are important:

- Deepens teacher's understanding of the mistaken goal chart.
- Significantly increases number and breadth of tools teachers have available for responding to misbehavior.
- Invites a sense of community when teachers understand that others have similar challenges.
- Reminds teachers that mistakes are opportunities to learn.
- Creates strong collaborative relationships for a teaching team.

In this section you will find:

- A one-page guide listing the steps of the Teachers Helping Teachers Problem Solving process.
- A longer version of the process that explains each step in more detail.

Moving it forward:

The problem-solving process can be done by reading and working through the step- by step description, however most find that additional training is very helpful. Many Certified Positive Discipline Trainers are available to train and support school staff to effectively use this process.

Tips:

When using the Teachers Helping Teachers Problem Solving Steps:

- Follow the steps.
- Use very specific, first person problems.
- Stay with the specific event.
- Avoid talking about the history.
- Avoid analyzing.
- Make sure that suggestions are given to the scribe,
- Do both role-plays.

We must realize that *we cannot build on deficiencies, only on strength.* We cannot help our children – or anyone else – to have faith in themselves as long as we have no faith in them.

- Dreikurs S*ocial Equality: The Challenge of Today*, p. 122 (emphasis in original)

Teacher Helping Teacher Problem-Solving Steps

Lynn Lott and Jane Nelsen

1. Explain the process (problem solving, real first-person problem, role play, solutions) and ask for a volunteer.
2. On a chart, record teacher's name, grade level, number of students in class, fictional name (for confidentiality) and age of challenging student.
3. State the problem in a one-line caption. (What would the headline be?)
4. Describe the last time the problem happened with enough detail so the group can get an idea of exactly what happened, as if describing a movie script. "What did you say and do? What did the student say and do? … Then what happened?"
5. Ask the teacher, "What were you thinking? How did you feel?" Refer to the Mistaken Goal Chart. Ask group if anyone else ever felt that way.
6. Using the teacher's feelings as the key, try to guess the belief behind the student's behavior.
7. Ask volunteer if she/he would be willing to try something more effective.
8. Set up role-play. Invite volunteer to play role of student. Ask for volunteers for other parts as needed. Role-play need not be more than 1 minute.
9. Process role-play by asking each player what he or she was thinking, feeling and deciding (to do) as the person he or she role-played.
10. Ask group to brainstorm (without discussing or analyzing) suggestions the volunteer could try. Record all suggestions. Volunteer just listens.
11. Ask volunteer to choose one suggestion he or she would be willing to try.
12. Do a second role-play using the suggestion, asking volunteer to play whichever role would be most helpful (him/herself or the student). Process thoughts, feelings and decisions of each major role player as above. If you have a group playing other students, you can ask what they noticed.
13. Ask for a commitment from the volunteer to try the suggestion for one week and report back.
14. Ask the group to share appreciations for what they learned from the process and for the volunteer.

Teachers Helping Teachers Problem-Solving Steps – Detail

Lynn Lott and Jane Nelsen

The Teachers Helping Teachers Problem-Solving Steps process is an effective and powerful practice that allows teachers to work with peers to solve nagging classroom problems. Teachers "grow their toolbox" for effective responses and often feel encouraged and empowered by the process. In our experience, teachers using these steps as a team quickly improve their skills using the Mistaken Goal Chart and gain helpful insight into the world of their students. Going through the steps with other teachers can be fun and invite helpful collaboration. It eliminates the endless analysis and looking for causes that lead to blame and excuses without helpful action.

1. *Explain the process (problem solving, real first-person problem, role play, solutions) and ask for a volunteer.*

- Introduce Teacher Helping Teachers Problem-Solving steps by telling the group that this is a process meant to help teachers increase their repertoire of effective responses while receiving help with a real challenge.
- The process involves inviting a volunteer to share a real, recent, first-person challenge (the volunteer's own challenge with a student) which has not been solved.
- The challenge will be described and then role-played before the group works on suggesting solutions. Not only will the volunteer get help, but observers will also see something of themselves and their own students in the situation and will get helpful insights and suggestions.
- Ask for a volunteer and then invite him or her to sit next to you. The volunteer teacher sits next to you because he/she is a co- teacher with you in this process. This way you can offer encouragement with your friendly energy. Also, you need to be close enough to convey in a friendly manner when you need to interrupt.

2. *Welcome the volunteer teacher. On a flip chart write the volunteer teacher's name, teaching grade level, and number of students in class. Write the challenging student's fictitious name, and age of the student.*

3. *Ask for a brief statement (a one-word or one-sentence headline) of the problem.*

In this step, you are looking for a general idea of the problem, not the details. Sometimes the teacher may give too much detail. Interrupt and say, "Later you will provide details. For now, if this challenge was a headline in a newspaper, what would it be?"

4. *Ask the teacher to describe the last time the problem occurred in enough detail and dialogue (like a movie script) that the group can get an idea of how to role-play the situation. If the volunteer needs help describing the situation, ask, "What did you do?" "What did the student do?" "Then what happened?" "What happened next?"*

- At this point, you are looking for the step-by-step story of the problem the last time it occurred. Unless you focus on the specifics of the one incident, you, the teacher, and everyone involved will become overwhelmed and leave without satisfactory help.
- One episode represents a microcosm of what occurs between this teacher and student. Focusing on and understanding the single incident will help other teachers with similar situations.
- Ask for a description that includes details and dialogue for role-players. This helps the teacher focus on the incident instead of telling stories about background and causes. Background details are a distraction to this process. Those details could be discussed forever without focusing on solutions.
- Sticking to the steps as outlined keeps the focus on finding a solution for a specific incident that brings clarity to the whole.

- Specifics are important because they help you find more clues about the mistaken goal. What the teacher did and the student's response to what the teacher did provide insight into the belief behind the student's behavior (of which he or she may not be consciously aware). For example,
    - If the student stops the behavior for a while in response to what the teacher did but starts up again a few moments or hour later, the belief behind the behavior is likely "I belong when I'm the center of attention" and the mistaken goal is probably undue attention.
    - If the student resists cooperation (actively or passively), the belief behind the behavior is likely "I belong when I'm the boss" and the goal is likely misguided power.

5. *Ask the teacher, "What did you think when this happened?" "When you thought that, what is one word that describes how you felt?" (If the volunteer has difficulty expressing a one-word feeling, refer him/her to the second column of the Mistaken Goal Chart and ask him/her to choose the group of feelings that fits.) Ask the group, "How many of you have ever felt that way?" (This is important so that the volunteer knows that he/she is not alone.)*

- Most people are not used to identifying their feelings. Explain that it takes only one word to describe a feeling. If this is an ongoing problem consider using a feeling faces chart and/or doing an activity to build emotional vocabulary with your staff such as "Glad, Sad, Mad, Scared" in *Positive Discipline in the School and Classroom Teachers' Guide: Activities for Students.*
- If the teacher is going on and on about what he/she thinks instead of what he/she feels, or if he/she comes up with a vague feeling such as "frustrated," use the Mistaken Goal Chart and ask the teacher to find a feeling in the second column that comes closest to describing his/her own.
- ***Ask for a show of hands of who in the group has experienced similar feelings.*** It is very encouraging for the volunteer teacher to not feel alone or inadequate. Knowing others are or have been in the same boat is reassuring.

6. *Based on the feeling expressed, guess the student's belief behind behavior and mistaken goal using the Mistaken Goal Chart.*

- It is important for the teacher to express feelings, because feelings give us clues about the belief behind the student's behavior, which we call the student's mistaken goal.
- If appropriate, you can explain that the adult's feeling is the key to understanding the belief behind the behavior. For example, if the teacher feels annoyed, this is a clue that the student's belief might be "I believe I belong when I'm the center of attention" and the mistaken goal would be Undue Attention.
- Some people get this confused and think you have to know what the student feels in order to understand his/her goal.
- Don't spend a lot of time trying to figure out the belief or goal. You are just making a guess and will get more information from the role-play. Even if you never know for sure what the mistaken goal is, people will get help from role-playing and brainstorming.

7. *Ask, "Would you be willing to try something else that would be more effective?"*

- This question is important to verify, clarify, and substantiate a commitment. It is a respectful agreement to move forward.
- Once in a while a teacher might say something like, "I have already tried everything." With a friendly smile, say something like, "It can certainly seem that way sometimes. Would you like to go exploring to discover if there might be a useful idea?" If the answer is no (extremely rare), and the teacher does not show a willingness to try something else, do not go further. Thank him/her for sharing this much and stop the process.

8. *Set up a role-play of the scene that was described by asking for volunteers to play each part. (Remember that the role-play need not take longer than one or two minutes to give all the information needed.)*

- Invite the teacher to play the role of the student so she/he can see the world through the eyes of the student. Ask for volunteers to play the parts of others described in the challenge. Have four to six people represent students in the classroom. This is important to show that even bystanders are affected by what goes on. The role-play is not meant to be improvisation. As much as possible stick to the original script and dialogue they heard during the description of the problem.
- Some facilitators are afraid that people will object to role-playing, and some people do. The resistance won't discourage a facilitator who is confident about the value of role-playing.
- Proceed to set up the role-play with confidence. When you ask for volunteers to play roles, be quiet and wait. Someone will fill the void of silence and volunteer. You might joke with them in your own way, or say, "I feel resistance. It reminds me of my resistance before I found out how valuable this is and how much fun it can be. Okay, who are the brave souls who are going to jump in and help me show how much fun this is?" Or simply, "I can wait."
- Set up the room to represent the real situation. Are the desks in rows or groupings? Is the teacher in the front of the room or somewhere else?
- To get the role-play started, remind someone of his or her opening line or ask the volunteer teacher to remind someone of an opening line.

9. *Process the role-play by asking players to share thoughts, feelings and decisions.*

- Stop the players as soon as you think they've had enough time to experience their thoughts, feelings and decisions (usually less than a minute).
- Ask the person playing the adult what he/she was thinking, feeling, and deciding. Then ask the "student" what he/she was thinking, feeling, and deciding. Finally turn to the group playing other students and invite any of them to share their thoughts, feelings, and decisions.
- This information sheds more light on the problem, and the processing serves as a debriefing for role-players who may be left with a lot of stirred-up feelings they need to express. Asking the students what they are deciding (to do) helps teachers see the long-term results of their actions instead of just the immediate result. Remember, feelings can usually be expressed in one word.

10. *Brainstorm with the group for possible solutions the teacher could try.*

- Brainstorming allows each person to participate. It helps people accept and value how easy it can be to solve other people's problems. When it's someone else's problem, we are not emotionally involved, so we have objectivity and perspective. Once we accept this, we can appreciate the value of being consultants to each other instead of thinking we should be able to solve all our own problems—or that we are failures if we even admit we are having a problem.
- Ask for a scribe to record all brainstormed suggestions on the flip chart. Suggestions should be written as stated. You might need to ask the person to state their suggestion concisely.
- It is helpful to place the flip chart away from the volunteer teacher and ask that comments be directed to the scribe instead of the volunteer.
- Tell the volunteer that they will surely hear suggestions that have been tried and to remain silent, remembering that the suggestions are really for all the teachers in the room and that putting all of the suggestions on the flip chart is helpful for everyone. *(Be sure every suggestion is written down.)*
- This is not a time for discussion or asking questions of the volunteer teacher, nor is it time to analyze any of the suggestions with the volunteer teacher.

- Encourage the group to think of as many alternatives as possible.
    - Ask everyone in the group to refer to the alternatives column of the "Mistaken Goal Chart" for ideas, or to make suggestions from their personal experience. You can also use the Positive Discipline tool cards to stimulate brainstorming.
    - Suggestions will improve as teachers learn more of the tools recommended in the books *Positive Discipline in the Classroom* and *Positive Discipline: A Teacher's A-Z Guide.* Do not censor negative suggestions.

11. *Ask the teacher to choose a suggestion to try for one week.*

- Read all the suggestions aloud, and then ask the volunteer to choose one he/she would be willing to try.
- Occasionally a teacher will say, "I've already tried all of them." Say something like, "Sounds like you really care and are trying everything you can think of. Would you be willing to pick one you have already tried, and we'll see what we can learn from the role-play about why it isn't working?"

12. *Set up a second role-play using the suggestion, asking volunteer to play whichever role would be most helpful (him/herself or the student). Process thoughts, feelings, and decisions of each major role player as above. If you have a group playing students, you can ask what they were thinking, feeling, and deciding.*

- Ask the teacher whether he/she would find practicing in the teacher or the student role more helpful. Ask him/her to take that role. (However, if a negative suggestion is chosen, be sure the teacher role-plays the student so that he/she can experience what the student might think, feel, and decide in response to that suggestion.)
- Some times the teacher will choose an idea that could be very effective but when he/she tries to apply it, some old habits (such as lecturing, controlling, throwing in a little humiliation) are incorporated and then it is less effective. All this will come out in the role-play, and those watching will also gain some insight about why some of the things they do may not be working.
- If the person role-playing does start lecturing or doing something other than the chosen suggestion, it is okay to interrupt and say, "Excuse me. What did you say you were going to do?" This almost always causes laughter from the role players and others as everyone sees how easy it is to get sidetracked into old habits. That is one reason why it is so important to role-play the suggestion.
- If the chosen suggestion is a negative one, the role-play will demonstrate why it doesn't work when you process the student's thoughts, feelings, and decisions. It is important to ask all role players what they were thinking, feeling, and deciding in order to learn how a situation affects everyone. Finding out that a chosen suggestion won't work doesn't mean the time has been wasted. Everyone will learn many valuable things during the process.
- If the suggestion did not produce positive results in the role-play, ask the teacher what he/ she learned from it. Ask if he/she would be willing to see what happens based on what was learned, and ask him/her to report back to the group next week. Many teachers find that they are able to be more creative the next time they encounter the problem because of what they learned during the Teachers Helping Teachers Problem-Solving Steps.

13. *Ask for the teacher's commitment to try the suggestion for one week and report back to the group at the following meeting.*

- Let the teacher know how important it is for the group to hear the results of his/her efforts so everyone can know how suggestions work in the real world. (We recommend regularly scheduled meetings for teachers, no less than once a month and preferably once a week while they are learning these new skills.)

14. *Ask the group for appreciations for the volunteer teacher.*

- Occasionally, participants want to keep teaching the volunteer. It is helpful to offer the following suggestions for appreciations:
    - This is the time to give back to the volunteer by telling him/her what this experience gave to you. Appreciations may sound like this: "I learned ___," "I felt____," "I have the same problem, so now I can try______," "I know how hard it is to share____."
    - What help did you get for yourself by watching this?
    - What did you see that you appreciate about the volunteer?
    - What ideas did you see that you could use?

Once teachers have become familiar with the expanded version, the short version provides an outline of the steps to be followed. Teachers may want to rotate the facilitator position so that everyone has an equal opportunity to have fun making mistakes while learning. The facilitator and every member of the group should have a copy of the Mistaken Goal Chart so they can refer to it when guessing the mistaken goal and when brainstorming for suggestions.

Moving it Forward (to be used only if you are knowledgeable about birth order):

- It can be fun to alert the group to some possibilities they could look for based on the birth order of the teacher and the student.
- For example, if the teacher is the oldest sibling in the family, are perfectionism and bossiness a problem? (Joke with the teacher: "We know you don't have these characteristics, but some other firstborn teacher might.") You might ask, "Are you sometimes too hard on yourself when things don't go as well as you would like?" This often helps a firstborn person feel understood. For those who are middle born, is trying to save the world a problem? They often see all sides to every issue and get caught up in what's fair. They often work well with rebels and underdogs. For teachers born last in their family, is a lack of order a problem, or are they waiting for someone else to fix things for them? They often allow for lots of creativity. A teacher who is an only child may be similar to an oldest or youngest. Ask only-children teachers if they sometimes have difficulties with students who fight or disagree with each other or borrow items without asking permission. You can also make some guesses about the student based on birth order. Is a youngest child looking for special service, a middle child looking for a place by being different, an oldest child giving up because he or she can't be first, or an only child having trouble sharing? There may not be time to spend on this issue, but it is helpful if facilitators are aware of it.

Handouts

In this section you will find:

- Handouts that accompany most of the activities in the Positive Discipline in the Classroom workshop.
- You may copy these handouts for your staff as long as the source at the bottom of the page is included.

Kindness and firmness at the same time

The "mis" behavior that you see is really the child's unskilled solution to another problem (that you may not see.)

CONNECT
B4
CORRECT

Where did we ever get the crazy idea that in order to make children do better, first we have to make them feel worse? CHILDREN DO BETTER WHEN THEY FEEL BETTER. - Jane Nelsen

We must convey loudly and clearly that, although some of their behaviors may be unacceptable, they are decent, worthwhile human beings and that we know they can make it and we will stick by them.

- Gootman, *The Caring Teacher's Guide to Discipline,* P. 10

Chart of Classroom Interventions by Mistaken Goal

Jody McVittie

Undue Attention Might look like: goofing off clowning annoying behavior distracting behavior helpless behavior incompetence dawdling etc…	Acknowledge student and the expectations of the situation.	"I love you and ___." (Example: I care about you and will spend time with you later.") Redirect by assigning a task so child can gain useful attention. Use secret signal (nonverbal). Use an "I message" Stand close by Pass a written note Encourage Touch without words
	Do the unexpected	Turn out the lights Lower your voice Change your voice Talk to the wall Cease teaching temporarily
	Teach belonging skills	Use class meetings Teach small group skills Teach small group problem solving Set up routines Involve in contributing to the class
	Distract the student	Ask a favor Give choices Change the activity Ask a direct question Change the student's chair
	Minimize attention	Avoid special service Ignore
	Prevention	Acknowledge student quietly. Greet students Notice small things about students Show curiosity about students Lunch with students (all of them in rotation)
Misguided Power Might look like: Bossiness Arguing with teacher Refusing to do things Saying things are "stupid" Dawdling Incompetence (passive power) Doing things his/her way Being critical of others Obstructing etc.	Acknowledge the student and the needs of the situation.	Acknowledge the student's power Don't fight and don't give in. Redirect to positive power by asking for help Offer limited choices Be firm and kind State both viewpoints Schedule a conference (with the student) Require a "re – entry" plan Let routines be the boss
	Make a graceful exit	Withdraw from conflict Leave and calm down Table the matter Remove the audience Take a teacher time out Act, don't talk Decide what you will do
	Use power positively	Class room jobs Leadership opportunities Have them tutor a younger child Ask for their ideas (esp. privately)
	Teach belonging and significance skills	Class meetings Follow through and using agreements

		Encourage positive power (Leadership and contribution)
	Prevention	Don't grab the bait Develop mutual respect Set a few reasonable limits Encouragement
Revenge Might look like: Saying hurtful things Damaging things Hurting kids Stealing/lying Obstructing in hurtful way	Acknowledge the student and the needs of the situation	Acknowledge hurt feelings Share your feelings Avoid feeling hurt Avoid punishment and retaliation Show you care Act don't talk Use reflective listening Do not protect from natural consequences
	Teach recovery skills	Teach apologies (whole class) Teach about making amends ("What can be done to fix this mistake?") Use class meetings Positive time out until student feels better
	Teach problem solving skills	Bugs and wishes "I messages" Self initiated "cool down time" Class meetings Teach internal monitoring as a science project
	Prevention tools	Build trust Use reflective listening
Assumed Inadequacy Might look like: (This one is more of a challenge because other mistaken goals can masquerade as inadequacy) Very discouraged but with low energy Need to get it right…and be so far from the mark that it isn't worth trying. Invisible Silent, attempts not to be noticed Very discouraged in a passive, hopeless way	Acknowledge the student and the needs of the situation	Have faith in child's abilities Break task down to small steps Stop all criticism Encourage any positive attempt Teach skills/show how, but don't do for Provide academic skills support (tutoring)
	Teach self encouragement skills	Model noticing change. Model making mistakes as an opportunity to learn. Model not being perfect Encourage, encourage, encourage Ask "what" and "how" questions. Focus on assets. Guide student to use assets to handle challenges. Compliments at class meetings (Giving and receiving). Class meeting brainstorm of "getting unstuck strategies" (for everyone) Set up opportunities for success Teach strategies for becoming "un-stuck.." Outlaw "I cant's" (with humor).
	Prevention	Build on student's interests. Don't pity Don't give up Enjoy the child Encourage, encourage, encourage

Adapted by Jody McVittie from: Nelsen, Jane — Positive Discipline
Albert, Linda — Cooperative Discipline
Dreikurs, Rudolf and Vicki Stolz — Children the Challenge

Encouragement vs. Praise Handout

From *Positive Discipline* (2006) Jane Nelsen, adapted by Jody McVittie

Encouragement

1. To inspire with courage
(courage < Old French *corage*, < Latin *cor* heart)
2. To spur on: to stimulate

Self-evaluation
("Tell me about it.")
("What do you think?")

Addresses Deed
Appreciation, Respectful
("Thank you for helping.")
("Who can show me the proper way to sit?")

Empathy
("What do you think and feel?")
("I can see that you enjoyed that.")

Self disclosing "I" messages
("I appreciate your help.")

Asks questions
("What is an appropriate noise level for the library?")

Effect:
Feel worthwhile without the approval of others.
Self confidence, Self reliance
Self esteem

Praise

1. To express a favorable judgment of
2. To glorify, especially by attribution of perfection.
3. An expression of approval

Evaluation by others
("I like it.")

Addresses doer
Expectation, Patronizing
("Your are such a good boy.")
("Good girl!")
("I like the way Suzie is sitting.")

Conformity
("You did it right.")
("I am so proud of you.")

Judgmental "I" messages
("I like the way you are sitting.")

Should statements
("You should be quiet like your sister.")

Effect:
Feel worthwhile only when others approve.
Dependence on others
"Other" esteem

Questions you might ask:
Am I inspiring self-evaluation or dependence on the evaluation of others?
Am I being respectful or patronizing?
Am I helping them discover how to act or trying to manipulate their behavior?
Am I seeing the child's point of view or my own?
Would I make this comment to a friend or neighbor?

Descriptive Encouragement: "I notice…" (without value judgments like good, well, or nice)
Appreciative encouragement: "I appreciate…." or, "Thank you for….."
Empowering encouragement: "I have faith in you…" or, "I trust you to…"

Courage (from the root word: *cor* – Latin, heart) is the very small step you take towards being more of who you truly are, when it might be easier to take a step in another direction. So when you encourage someone, you are creating a space for him or her to take that step toward his/her best self.

De-escalation Tips: For When the Mid-brain Takes Over

Rx for the Flipped Lid

From *Conflict Unraveled: Fixing Problems at Work and in Families* by Andra Medea, adapted by Jody McVittie

We refer to this as **"having a flipped lid" or "flooding."**

Tips for when YOU have flipped your lid:

- **Recognize what it feels like physically**: fast heartbeats, pounding head, a sense of urgency, etc. Learn your own body's warning signs.
- **Recognize what it feels like mentally**: a sense of urgency, thoughts that keep repeating or going in circles, an inability to think calmly and clearly (or do mental math). Learn your own mind's warning signs.
- **Take a time-out from the situation to calm down**. Recognize that continued engagement isn't going to help.
- **Focus on your breathing**. Do belly breathing.
- **Use large muscles**: Walk, do isometrics, do windmills with your arms.
- **Try to engage your cortex.** Do mental math, spell things backwards, list facts…and slow the pace.
- **Notice why you are in "survival brain.**" "This situation makes me feel vulnerable because. . . " (I'm not being heard, I may not be able to prevent injury, I'm not being respected) and work to not take it personally.

Tips for when the OTHER person has flipped his/her lid (child or adult):

- **Watch for signs in the other person**: Irrational action, flushed face, intense emotion, disjointed sentences.
- **Notice your own body.** Remember that mirror neurons work quickly. Don't let the other person's flipped lid "catch" you.
- **Remember safety.** People who are using their mid-brain and not their cortex do not act rationally and can be physically dangerous. Stay calm, move slowly, and be aware.
- **Use your mirror neurons.** The more you stay calm and connected, the easier it is for the other person to calm down.
- **Acknowledge feelings:** Use few words and a calm, empathetic tone.
- **Don't talk at the person.** Don't touch, and don't make fast movements. If he/she wants to leave (and it is safe) allow it.
- **Don't crowd.** Don't make demands; don't give complicated directions (a person with a flipped lid cannot process complex verbal statements).
- **Invite the person to take a time-out (non punitive) or "cool down time" (CDT)** This works best if it is an option, not a command.
- **Simple tasks may engage the cortex**. You might ask him/her to remind you how his/her name is spelled, to count to ten, ask if he/she remembers how to spell your name.
- **Ask for his/her help**. After the student has begun to de-escalate, change the subject by asking for his/her help. "I can tell you aren't ready to engage in work yet, but are you calm enough to help me by…?" "I can tell you aren't quite ready to play again, but would you be willing to help me by…?"

Focus on Solutions

No More Logical Consequences (At Least Hardly Ever. . .)

Jane Nelsen

During a class meeting, students in a fifth grade class were asked to brainstorm logical consequences for two students who didn't hear the recess bell and were late for class. Following is their list of "consequences:"

1. Make them write their names on the board.
2. Make them stay after school that many minutes.
3. Take away that many minutes from tomorrow's recess.
4. No recess tomorrow.
5. The teacher could yell at them.

The students were then asked to forget about consequences and brainstorm for solutions that would help the students be on time. Following is their list of solutions:

1. Someone could tap them on the shoulder when the bell rings.
2. Everyone could yell together, "Bell!"
3. They could play closer to the bell.
4. They could watch others to see when they are going in.
5. Adjust the bell so it is louder.
6. They could choose a buddy to remind them that it is time to come in.

The difference between these two lists is profound. The first looks and sounds like punishment. It focuses on the past and making kids "pay" for their mistake.

The second list looks and sounds like solutions that focus on "helping" the kids do better in the future. It focuses on seeing problems as opportunities for learning. It other words, the first list is designed to hurt, the second is designed to help.

In the first list, the kids try to disguise punishment by calling it a logical consequence. Why do they do that? Could it be that this is what they are learning from adults? The Four Rs of Logical Consequences (Related, Respectful, Reasonable, and Revealed in advance) were conceived in an attempt to stop the trend of logical consequences sounding like punishment, but they have not totally eliminated this problem.

Where did we ever get the crazy idea that in order to make children DO better first we have to make them FEEL worse? When people first hear this quote from "Positive Discipline," they usually laugh as they think about how it doesn't make sense. However, when it comes to act, it seems that parents, teachers, and students have difficulty accepting that people do better when they feel better.

For example, many teachers like Nos. 2 and 3 on the first list above, ("Make them stay after school that many minutes," and "Take away that many minutes off tomorrow's recess.") It is true that those suggestions are related, reasonable, and could be enforced respectfully and revealed in advance. However, they all focus on making the child pay for the past mistake instead of finding a solution to solve the problem in the future. In other words, they are designed to make the children feel bad in the hopes that that will motivate them to do better. Punishment often stops misbehavior, but it hardly ever motivates children to do better in the future — unless they are approval junkies. Instead, they are motivated to rebel, get revenge, or to be more careful about getting caught.

Kay Rogers, a recently retired teacher from Sharon School in North Carolina said, "After I heard about the possibility of focusing on solutions instead of consequences, it was the hardest habit for me to break. All my life I had believed that kids learned from punishment -- or at least from consequences. I can now see that my students and I both tried to disguise punishment by calling it consequences -- even though the consequences weren't as harsh as blatant punishment. I had to learn about the effectiveness of focusing on solutions right along with my students. We were all surprised by the difference it made in our classroom. The level of respect and caring for each other was raised ten fold. Students became pleased to find their name on the agenda because they knew, as Jane Nelsen had told us, that we would have a whole room full of consultants to give them valuable suggestions. And, the solutions they found were much more effective in changing behavior than anything we had done before."

This does not mean logical consequences cannot be effective when properly understood and appropriately used. Hopefully the chapter on Natural and Logical Consequences in the newly revised edition of *Positive Discipline* will help. However, logical consequences are rarely necessary and are only one possibility. Rudolph Dreikurs taught that logical consequences are effective ONLY for the mistaken goal of undue attention (and are only one option even for that goal). Too many adults look for logical consequences "to punish" every behavior. Looking for solutions is more effective in most situations.

> Solutions are Related, Respectful, Reasonable *and* HELPFUL.

Many teachers have switched and now teach the Three Rs and an H for Solutions: Related, Respectful, Reasonable and HELPFUL. Once students have brainstormed for solutions to a problem, it is extremely important to let the individual student choose the solution he or she thinks will be most helpful. A vote should be taken only if the problem involves the whole class.

Of course, focusing on solutions instead of consequences is also more effective in homes. One parent said, "I can't believe how many power struggles I created by trying to impose 'logical consequences'. We have so much more peace in our home now that we focus on solutions."

The chapter on logical consequences in Positive Discipline explains when and how to use effective logical consequences. However, in most cases, it is much simpler and much more helpful to focus on solutions.

Helpful Hints for Empowering vs. Enabling Handout

Jane Nelsen and Lynn Lott, adapted by Jody McVittie.

We have become vividly aware of how skilled most of us are at offering enabling responses to students, and how unskilled we are at offering empowering responses.

Our definition of *enabling* is: "Getting between young people and life experiences to minimize the consequences of their choices." Enabling responses include:

- Doing too much for them
- Giving them too much
- Overprotecting/rescuing
- Lying for them
- Punishing/controlling
- Living in denial
- Fixing
- Bailing them out

Our definition of *empowering* is: "Turning control over to young people as soon as possible so they have power over their own lives." Empowering responses include:

- Listening and giving emotional support and validation without fixing or discounting
- Teaching life skills
- Working on agreements through class meetings or the joint problem-solving process
- Letting go (without abandoning)
- Deciding what you will do with dignity and respect
- Sharing what you think, how you feel, and what you want (without lecturing, moralizing, insisting on agreement, or demanding that anyone give you what you want)
- Sticking to the issue with dignity and respect

More hints:

- Enabling responses tend to be easier for most of us than empowering responses. The empowering statements may seem awkward.
- Punishment is enabling, not because of the lack of firmness, but because
  - Control remains with the adult
  - The focus moves from the problem to a power/revenge relationship between the adult and child
  - The young person often believes he/she has "made the payment" and therefore can drop the problem
  - The young person and adult can shift their focus to resentment instead of problem solving
  - The young person no longer takes responsibility for finding a solution

Note: The full activity and statements are included later in this manual.

Making Agreements and Following Through Handout

From "Follow Through With Teens" in *Teaching Parenting the Positive Discipline Way*, 5th edition, Lynn Lott and Jane Nelsen

The Steps of Making an Agreement

1. Have a friendly discussion with the other person to gather information about what is happening regarding the problem. Start by owning your part of the problem. (Listen and be mutually respectful.)

2. Brainstorm possible solutions. Chose a mutually agreeable solution. This may take some negotiating because each person may have a different favorite. Be willing to learn from mistakes. (Notice that there is no threat or "consequence" here. Consequences undermine the power of any agreement.)

3. Agree on a specific time deadline (to the minute).

4. At the deadline, you simply follow through on the agreement by firmly and respectfully requesting the other person to keep the agreement until it is done.

Four Hints for Effective Follow Through

1. Keep comments simple and concise. ("I notice you didn't _____. Would you please do that now?")

2. In response to objections ask, "What was our agreement?"

3. In response to further objections, shut your mouth and use nonverbal communication (point to your watch; smile knowingly; give a hug and point to your watch again).

4. When the other person concedes to keep to the agreement (sometimes obviously annoyed) simply say, "Thank you for keeping our agreement."

Four Traps that Defeat Follow Through

1. Wanting other people to have the same priorities as you do.

2. Getting into judgments and criticism rather than sticking to the issue.

3. Not getting specific agreements in advance that include a specific time deadline.

4. Not maintaining dignity and respect for the other person and yourself.

Positive Discipline in the Classroom Management Tools

(Tools to Avoid Punishment, Rescuing, Controlling, Power Struggles, Revenge)

Jane Nelsen & Lynn Lott.

- *Ask* "what" and "how" questions instead of *telling* what, how, and why. Make sure you listen to what the student says
- Offer limited choices
- Act, don't talk
- Use few words (1-10)
- Write a post-it note
- Connect before correct
- Special time
- Use humor (respectfully)
- Mirror: "I notice…"
- Compliments
- Kind and firm
- Class meetings
- Wheel of Choice
- Decide what you will do
- Small steps
- Use nonverbal cues
- Message of caring
- Emotional honesty: "I feel…, because..., and I wish…."
- Encouragement instead of praise or rewards
- Jobs for a feeling of belonging and significance
- Positive time out (or cool-down space): Let students help design it
- See *mistakes as opportunities* for learning
- If you say it, mean it; and if you mean it follow through with respect and dignity
- Understand the belief behind the behavior: Use perception modification instead of behavior modification
- Joint problem-solving with mutually agreeable deadlines.
- Go beyond consequences – brainstorm for solutions.
- Do nothing – allow natural consequences
- "You can figure it out; come back with your plan."
- Use friendly eyes/smile and nonverbal signals

"What" and "How" Curiosity Questions Handout

Jane Nelsen & Lynn Lott, adapted by Teresa LaSala

Tone is important. Interest and caring must be expressed through tone.

- What happened?
- What would you like to have happen?
- What or how did you contribute to that outcome?
- How can you be helpful? What would you like to do to help?
- What do you think caused that to happen?
- How did your choices impact the outcome?
- What were you trying to accomplish?
- How do you feel about what happened?
- What did you learn from this experience?
- What ideas do you have to take care of this problem?
- What could you do next time?
- How could you solve this?
- How can you use what you learned in the future?
- What do you think will happen if you take that course of action?
- What is your picture of…?
- What is your plan for …?
- How do you see that working…?
- What is your story about …?
- What is your understanding of our agreement?
- What is your understanding of what I just said?

One looks back with appreciation to the brilliant teachers, but with gratitude to those who touched our human feelings. The curriculum is so much necessary raw material, but warmth is the vital element for the growing plant and for the soul of the child.

—Carl Jung

Classroom and School Strategies

Quick Summary:
There are many applications for Positive Discipline in your classroom and school. Included here are some practical tools that others have used to invite further discussion and apply Positive Discipline solutions.

In this section you will find:

- A Positive Discipline approach to helping students work more effectively with guest teachers/substitutes.
- A template for discussion about responses to behavior
- A template and survey to monitor progress on how your school is moving toward implementing Positive Discipline.

Moving it forward:

- We'd love to know how you have taken this work deeper. Have you painted a wheel of choice on the playground? Send us pictures.
- Have you used Positive Discipline tools to run an effective student council that takes on real problems? Share your stories with us!
- What else has your classroom created?
- What else have you learned?
- Become part of our community and help us grow the work.

"If you want to build a ship, don't drum up the people to gather wood, divide the work, and give orders. Instead, teach them to yearn of the vast and endless sea."

– Antoine de Saint Exupery

Strategies for Substitutes: Respect and the "Guest Teacher"

Jody McVittie

Having a substitute teacher for a day can be a nightmare--for the students, for the regular teacher, and for the substitute. Several steps can make these days a much better experience.

1) Recognize what happens from the students' point of view.

- Students have a strong positive relationship with their teacher. When the teacher is not present they can feel abandoned, betrayed, or hurt. This invites hurtful behavior that can be aimed at peers and /or the guest teacher.
- Sometimes, students behave well for their regular teacher because they are afraid of what the teacher may do "to" them but have not internalized the socially appropriate behavior. As a result, when the teacher is absent, their behavior may change dramatically.
- Sometimes students create mischief because it is fun to collaborate with each other and working toward a common goal (though it is not helpful to the substitute) creates an engaging sense of connection.

2) Plan for guest teachers using multiple strategies.

- Whenever possible, let students know ahead of time that you will be absent, and that there will be a guest teacher.
- Let students know that you would **prefer to be in the classroom because you care about** them. You will do your best to make sure the guest teacher has the information he/she needs.
- When you can't let the students know ahead of time, leave a short note for the guest teacher to read to your students.
- Consider having a place for students to leave notes for you in case they have messages to communicate. Commit to reading those before class starts the day you return.
- When you know which substitute works well for your classroom, have her/him return if possible. Students appreciate your efforts to make their day successful.

3) Develop a classroom procedure for guest teachers *with the students* ahead of time.

If you are doing class meetings, go to Role-playing and Brainstorming: Working with Guest Teachers, *Positive Discipline in the School and Classroom Teachers' Guide: Activities for Students.* If you have not yet started class meetings, you can engage students by holding a discussion. Tips:

- Let students know that occasionally there will be a guest teacher.
- Reflect on what happens daily in the classroom.
- Brainstorm different ways they can bother a guest teacher (write them down) then reflect on what it might feel like to be the guest teacher. Role-play one or two of the suggestions. Students can then brainstorm ways to make the day better for both the substitute and the students.
- Ask students to imagine what it would be like to have a different teacher in the classroom for a day.
    - What were you feeling?
    - What might be different?
    - What might be hard or what might be fun?
    - What would make it easier for you?
    - What would you like the substitute to know about you or about our class?
- Have students imagine *being* the substitute.
    - What might you feel walking into the classroom?
    - What might be hard? What might be fun?
    - What would make it easier for the substitute?
- Another solution-focused prompt is: "How can we invite our guest teacher to feel welcome in our classroom?" Typical student responses to this include:
    - Make morning announcements that welcome and remind the students about guest teachers
    - Have nametags that the students wear.
    - Have a book with a list of student jobs.

  - Have a book with a list of class guidelines and procedures.
  - Have a welcoming committee. Have students get specific about the welcomer's job. (Introductions, class tour, materials, explaining routines etc.)
- Role-play one or more of these ideas to help students understand and practice.

4) **Develop a plan for assessing how the day went with the guest teacher.** Students will have lots of ideas:
- The class can create a reflection form for the guest teacher. (Ideas for this could be a homework project.)
- The class can create a self-reflection form for students. (Sample below.)

5) **Make the plan work.**
- Let the guest teacher know that the class is working on welcoming him or her.
- Inform the guest teacher about classroom routines and how your class solves problems.
- Follow through with your agreements with the class. Let them know ahead of time whenever possible; leave a letter; keep the "guest teacher" book available; have a place for notes to you; and review and discuss self-reflection forms.

Ideas from guest teachers who have been successful and enjoy their work:
- Acknowledge openly at the beginning of class that it is tough when your regular teacher is absent.
- Take time to introduce and share something about yourself.
- Allow the students to introduce and say something about themselves. Try to learn their names.
- If you believe students are playing games with names, be straight with them. (E.g., "I'm guessing from the laughter that there is some fun with names going on. I personally prefer to be known by my real name, but if you'd rather have a different identity today, it is ok with me. The really important thing is that you can learn with the name that you choose.")
- Work hard to see the students for who they are, not what they do.

"Substituting behaviors" -a true story from Elk Grove School District, contributed by Jane Nelsen:

A counselor used the issue of substitutes during a class meeting with fourth grade students by asking the kids, "What do you do to 'bug a sub?'" The kids got a kick out of sharing all the things they did such as changing names, book drops, making fun of the substitute. All their sharing was recorded on a flip chart.

The next question was, "How do you think the substitute feels when these things are being done?"

It was interesting to watch the kids think about this as though they had never thought about it before. They had heard lectures about how rude they were, but they had never been invited to think about it. They started volunteering their ideas about how the things they did must make the substitute feel angry, hurt, and sad.

The counselor then asked, "How many of you would be willing to help the substitute instead of hurting him or her?" They all raised their hand, so the counselor asked, "What could you do to help?"

Every suggestion the kids brainstormed was very respectful, such as help her feel welcome, show her where things are, give our correct names, think about her feelings, be respectful.

The kids followed through on their ideas. The next time there was a substitute she left a note for the regular teacher that she had never been treated so respectfully.

Sample Guest Teacher Checklist

Kay Kummerow from *The Adlerian Resource Book,* adapted by Jody McVittie

To my students:
I'm sorry that I cannot be with you in class today. Please record your behavior and academic progress for today. (Circle yes or no, or answer with a sentence.)

1. Did you smile at the guest teacher when you walked in the door? Yes No
2. Did you say hello? Yes No
3. What is the guest teacher's name? ______________________
4. Have you had this teacher before in another class? Yes No
5. Were you in your seat when the tardy bell rang? Yes No
6. Did you help with attendance? Yes No
7. Did you listen to the directions for the lessons? Yes No
8. Did you understand the directions? Yes No
9. Did you ask a question about the directions? Yes No
10. What question did you ask?

11. Were you surprised when you saw that I was absent today? Yes No
12. Did you remember that I told you I would be absent today? Yes No
13. Today I'm at a workshop. What do you think I want to learn about?

14. Are you surprised to learn that teachers also learn? Yes No
15. Would you be interested in hearing about my workshop? Yes No
16. Were you a cooperative and helpful member of the class today? Yes No
17. What did you do to help make this a good class today?

18. Do you think that this guest teacher will want to teach our class again? Yes No
19. Why or why not?

20. List five (5) things you learned today.

We learn best from those with whom we are in caring, mutually respectful relationships that promote independence. Such supportive relationships enable students from diverse backgrounds to feel comfortable bringing their personal experiences into the classroom, discover their common humanity and feel as though they are viewed as assets to the school community.

Learning First Alliance *Every Child Learning: Safe and Supportive Schools*

Decision Tree for Adult Responses

From: BRIDGES by Lois Ingber, Jody McVittie

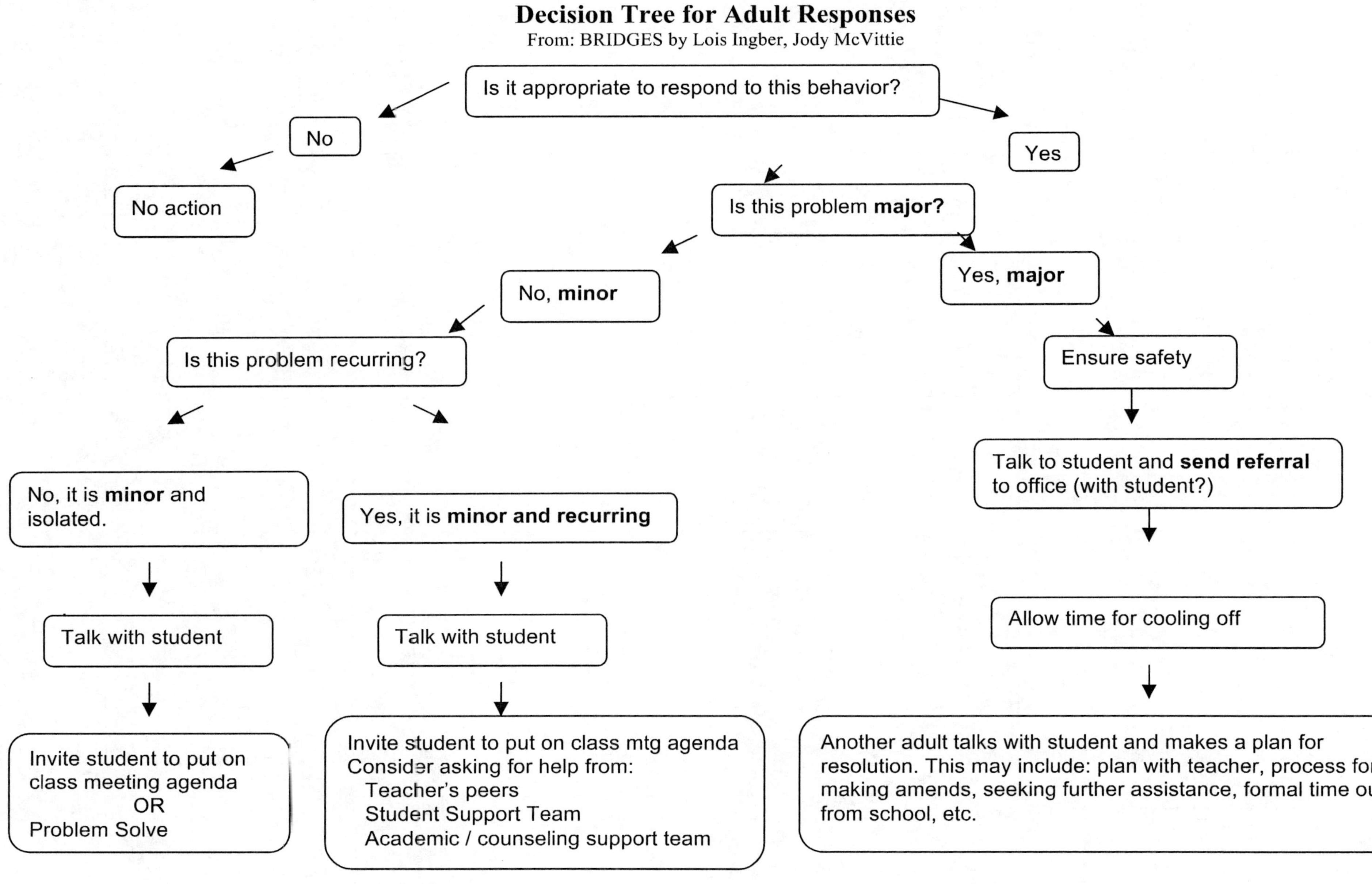
Is it appropriate to respond to this behavior?
No
No action
Yes
Is this problem **major?**
No, **minor**
Is this problem recurring?
No, it is **minor** and isolated.
Talk with student
Invite student to put on class meeting agenda
OR
Problem Solve
Yes, it is **minor and recurring**
Talk with student
Invite student to put on class mtg agenda
Consider asking for help from:
Teacher's peers
Student Support Team
Academic / counseling support team
Yes, **major**
Ensure safety
Talk to student and **send referral** to office (with student?)
Allow time for cooling off
Another adult talks with student and makes a plan for resolution. This may include: plan with teacher, process for making amends, seeking further assistance, formal time out from school, etc.

A Developmental Continuum of Positive Discipline

(An awareness of the process of change)

Terry Chadsey

	A community of control	A community in transition	A community of mutual respect
Teachers / Parents			
Students / Children			
Class Meetings/ Family Meetings			
Problem Solving			
Response to mistakes			
Responsibility			
Class Jobs/Family work			
Collaboration with community			

ID: ____________________

Continuum Toward a Positive Discipline Classroom

Teachers learning to implement Positive Discipline in the Classroom have asked, "How do I know when my class is being successful?" This questionnaire is designed to offer specific guide points for moving toward a more democratic classroom. The statements and your responses may offer you insight into ways to help your students develop a greater sense of personal responsibility, belonging, value and academic engagement in your classroom. The goal, of course, is a thriving community that supports the maximum amount of learning and growth for each child.

If a statement does not apply to your class because of the grade you teach, mark it NA. If you are unfamiliar with a term or concept used in a statement, mark it DK. Rate your classroom using the following scale:

1	2	3	4	5
No, we/I do not yet do this.	About 25% of the time we/I do this.	About 50% of the time we/I do this.	About 75% of the time we/I do this.	This is true of me/our class about 95% of the time.

Note: "secondary" refers to grades 6 and up

1. Class Meetings are held at least 3 times per week (in elementary) or at least once a week (in secondary).	1
2. At least 90% of the class members give compliments based upon helpfulness, accomplishments or sharing on a regular basis in Class Meetings.	2
3. Students demonstrate a high level of respect for self and others in problem solving by focusing on helpful solutions that are respectful to all concerned (as opposed to blame and punishment) in Class Meetings.	3
4. In grades 3 and higher, students run the Class Meeting with minimal adult assistance.	4
5. Students maintain good eye contact when giving and receiving compliments.	5
6. Students respond with "Thank you" upon receiving a compliment (note: Secondary students might give a positive acknowledgement in some other appropriate form).	6
7. Students demonstrate appropriate eye contact with others when discussing problems and solutions.	7
8. Students demonstrate concern for fellow students and adults by listening respectfully during Class Meetings.	8
9. When someone is speaking during Class Meetings, interruptions are the exception rather than the rule, and are out of enthusiasm for sharing problem solving ideas or plans.	9
10. Students can identify several academic choices they have helped make in class or Class Meeting each week (elementary) /each month (secondary) such as curriculum content, due dates for projects or tests, and kinds of products to demonstrate learning.	10
11. Students have the opportunity each week (elementary) / each month (secondary) in Class Meetings to plan and make choices for free time, field trips, or special activities for the class.	11
12. Students can explain to a visitor the difference between the kinds of problems they should report to an adult, and the kinds of problems they should handle with the Class Meeting, Four Problem Solving Suggestions, or Wheel of Choice.	12
13. Students can work effectively in cooperative groups, learning, sharing responsibility and working out problems so that teacher involvement is focused on helping students with academic questions.	13
14. During teacher instruction time, student questions relate to academic pursuits; behavior	14

problems between students are handled appropriately by students using the Four Problem Solving Suggestions or Positive Time Out.	
15. Students take responsibility for their feelings in problem situations by using "I messages" (or similar format) in Class Meetings and in the classroom.	15
16. Students can state to a visitor at least 4 reasons for having Class Meetings.	16
17. There is a Positive Time Out Space in the classroom and students helped develop the guidelines for its use.	17
18. Voluntarily, or upon teacher direction, students use the Time Out Space as it is designed to be used.	18
19. Students spontaneously give compliments to other students at times other than the Class Meeting. (For this question, answer 1 if never, 2 if about once or twice a week, 3 if about once a day, 4 if about twice a day, and 5 if more frequently than twice a day).	19
20. There are enough classroom jobs for each student to have one at the elementary level, and they are rotated on a regular basis.	20
21. There are several classroom jobs at the secondary level and they are rotated on a regular basis.	21
22. When a student approaches me with a problem, I refrain from taking responsibility for solving the problem and instead ask "What" and "How" questions or cue the student to use the Class Meeting agenda, the Four Problem Solving Suggestions or the Wheel of Choice.	22
23. I use the Class Meeting agenda, the Problem Solving Suggestions and the Wheel of Choice myself for problem solving.	23
24. I use "What" and "How" questions to help students who need assistance with problem solving; I avoid "Why" questions as much as possible.	24
25. I model the use of Positive Time Out (either by using the class space or a space I have designated for myself) when I am upset.	25
26. I use "I messages" (or similar format) to take ownership of my own feelings in class and in the Class Meeting.	26
27. I can identify the Mistaken Goal for a student who is misbehaving and I can use proactive strategies based upon that Mistaken Goal.	27
28. I believe "Mistakes are Wonderful Opportunities to Learn" and I model the use of the "Four R's of Recovery" when I make a mistake with my students.	28
29. To prepare my students for Class Meetings, I have taught them the lessons included in "Preparing the Ground" and "8 Essential Skills for Effective Class Meetings" found in *Positive Discipline in the School and Classroom Teachers' Guide: Activities for Students.*	29
30. Students are included as active participants in Parent/Teacher/Student conferences.	30
31. At least ¾ of my positive comments to students (in feedback on papers or in verbal interaction) would fall into the category of "encouragement" rather than "praise."	31

Any additional comments you would like to make about the impact of PD in your classroom: ______

____

____

As we work to refine this questionnaire, there may come a day that someone can say to you that the sum of your ratings places you at a certain spot in the continuum of change to a Positive Discipline Classroom. That might, however, detract from the greater value of a questionnaire like this: the value of looking at ourselves at several points in time and thinking about specific ways we can move in a positive direction to help children grow to become more successful members of society.

Developed by: Suzanne J. Smitha, Positive Discipline Lead Trainer, with assistance from other associates. Reliability analyses: 3/1/02. Excel File available for further analysis of scores. Contact Suzanne at **asmitha@mindspring.com**.

Framework for Getting Started
Learning and Sharing the Principles of Positive Discipline in the School and Classroom

You are committed to the idea of implementing Positive Discipline in the Classroom and class meetings. How do you get started? If you want to share these practices with your school, what are your first steps? You can tailor the steps below for any situation by choosing the ones that fit for you.

1. **Begin by reviewing materials, with some time for personal reflection.**
   - Look through *Positive Discipline in the School and Classroom Teachers' Guide Activities for Students,* focusing on the blue face sheets.
   - Review your notes and handouts from the workshop.
   - *Agreements and guidelines.* What are the classroom agreements? Did my students help create them? Is there buy-in? How do my students perceive the climate of the classroom?
   - *Routines.* Are my routines clear and well established? Do my students understand them? Have we practiced?
   - *Meaningful work.* Do my students have classroom jobs?
   - *Self-regulation.* How do I self-manage when I'm feeling stressed? What do I do when my "lid is flipped."
   - Reflect: Who am I as leader? What are my next steps toward creating a classroom of cooperation?

2. **Start practicing with small *one-on-one interactions.*** Examples include:
   - *Communication skills:* Do vs. don't. Say what you want instead of what you don't want.
   - *Mutual Respect.* Begin with self-respect. Notice when you say, "Yes" (or don't say anything) when you really mean no.
   - *Building cooperation.* Ask more, tell less.
   - *Mistakes and how to fix them.* Practice modeling mistakes. Practice repairs.
   - *Encouragement.* Try encouragement more, praise less.
   - *Respecting differences.* Look for the belief behind the behavior. How is this student "saying" I want to belong, or I want to matter?

3. **Teach your students the skills using the activities in *Positive Discipline in the School and Classroom Teachers' Guide: Activities for Students.***
   - Review the section: *How to Use This Manual*
   - Proceed with teaching the concepts in order. It is an excellent page-by-page guide.

4. **Begin to share with interested colleagues.**
   - Remind yourself of what you learned from the Continuum of Change and Top Card. Not all teachers will welcome new information.
   - Be a role model for respectful interactions with students and colleagues.
   - Share one or two simple successes (for example, how one of your students responded to encouragement).
   - Start a book club using *Positive Discipline in the Classroom.*

5. **Connect with building leadership.**
   - Meet with your administrator and/or building leadership team. Share what you have learned and what you would like to do.
   - Offer to share a short activity with them and/or with the whole staff.

- Engage in a discussion with your leadership team. (See story below) Discussion topics might include:
    - the importance of social emotional learning (SEL),
    - the value of integrating discipline and the SEL program,
    - the benefit of having common language and process for a whole school approach,
    - how the school monitors/assesses culture and climate, and
    - the importance of having students practice the skills they are learning.

6. **With the support of your team, create a plan for bringing this work to your school. Ideas could include:**
    - Introduce concepts that have been useful to you at a faculty meeting by teaching short activities. See "So You've Agreed to Give a Presentation" (later in this handout) for some ideas on topics that can be presented in 15 minutes or less at a faculty meeting.
        - It is uncomfortable for adults to move from the unconscious to the conscious; remember the "Continuum of Change."
        - Take small steps by using encouragement and sharing practical success stories from your own classroom.
    - Start a Positive Discipline email list within your school so that you and your colleagues can share stories and experiences.
    - Start a *Teacher Helping Teacher Problem Solving* group that meets on a regular basis. You can use *Positive Discipline: A Teacher's A-Z Guide* as a resource.

7. As you generate more interest, **consider inviting a Certified Positive Discipline Trainer** to come do more training, or better yet, become a trainer yourself. For more information, visit the www.positivediscipline.org website under training/ certification.

A school story:
I was invited by the leadership team at an elementary school in Washington State to discuss using Positive Discipline at the school. The team wanted to have a clear understanding not only of what Positive Discipline could offer, but why they might choose to use it at their school.

The most pressing problem was that current interventions for students struggling the most with behavior were not working. The process regularly removed students from class or from the school but behavior was not improving. When invited to comment, I suggested that for these students, all of whom had been exposed to trauma, removing them from the situation, though sometimes helpful to other students, was not teaching them the skills they needed to be successful.

The team reflected and noticed that in their school, many of the students were missing significant social skills but that the teachers were so good at compensating they were able to teach… until they needed a substitute. This invited one more level of reflections. At this school, behavior seemed to get worse as the students got older. One brave educator commented that at home she expected her children's behavior to improve as they got older and wondered why the school seemed to have a different standard. Another team member commented that perhaps the younger children were behaving because they were afraid. As the students got older, they got bolder.

In summing up their discussion, the team noticed that in their valiant efforts to boost academic skills they were not supporting the students by having a solid framework for teaching and practicing the social skills that are so important for future success. As a first step, they planned to move forward by carefully evaluating the Positive Discipline program to ensure that it was consistent with their building goals.

-Jody McVittie

A Framework for Restarting Positive Discipline in the Classroom

Some teachers come to this work with extensive experience in Positive Discipline or teach at a school that has been using Positive Discipline, including regular structured class meetings. Doing the same activities year after year may be less interesting to you or to your students. Below is a process for a review to get the process re-started more quickly.

The blue-paged *face sheets* in *Positive Discipline in the School and Classroom Teachers' Guide* offer an explanation of what follows in each section, as well as the suggested order for activities. With experienced students and thoughtful review of the questions below, you should be able to pick activities that will be the most beneficial to your classroom. We recommend that you move your class through a number of activities based upon their skill levels and needs so that they can practice working together.

Preparing the Ground and Essential Skills for Class Meetings still matter. The following questions will help you assess your students' skill levels and guide you in selecting activities from each section of the *Positive Discipline in the School and Classroom Teachers' Guide*:

- *Agreements and guidelines:*
  - Have the students participated in designing the classroom agreements/guidelines?
  - Do you review the guidelines every 4-6 weeks to see if updates are needed?
- *Routines:*
  - Do the students know the routines?
  - Do you continue to practice them?
  - Are they skilled at handling routines when there are unexpected or unforeseen events?
- *Meaningful work:*
  - Do students have meaningful class jobs?
  - Are jobs modified to become more challenging as the year progresses?
  - Do they know what it means to do each job well?
- *Communication Skills:* Do they listen while others talk?
- *Mutual Respect:* Are students showing respect to themselves, each other and to you?
- *Building Cooperation:* Are all students included in cooperative learning tasks and cooperative activities during free choice?
- *Mistakes and How to Fix Them:* How effectively do students handle mistakes and apologies?
- *Encouragement:* How often do you hear words of encouragement between students?
- *Respecting* Differences: Is there a feeling of emotional safety and trust?
- *Compliments and Appreciations:*
  - Are compliments given directly in the first person?
  - Are compliments given for helpfulness and accomplishments?
- *Focusing on Solutions:*
  - Are students skilled at being helpful, not hurtful?
  - Can students focus on solutions?
- *Class Meetings:*
  - Is the equipment in place (notebook or box) for an agenda?
  - Is an object passed around the circle for giving compliments and brainstorming solutions?
  - Do students choose how to solve problems from three options (share feelings while others listen, discuss without fixing, or ask for problem solving help)?

You've Agreed to Give a Presentation - Now What?

Keep the information simple, practical, applicable, fun, experiential and real. When teachers receive help for situations they deal with every day, they'll want more. A lecture on discipline isn't as appealing as practical ideas on what to do when kids misbehave in the classroom.

Tips:

- Keep it short (10-15 minutes)
- Take small steps: teach pieces that a teacher new to the material could use without a huge paradigm shift.
- Don't try to change others. You are offering a gift – it is up to them whether they believe you that it works, or whether they choose to try a new tool. Recognize that you are planting seeds. Some may find fertile soil, others won't
- Know that there will be colleagues who might be threatened by the ideas, and remind them only to use what works for them in their classroom.

Some short topics that have worked to begin to introduce Positive Discipline Concepts:

- Asking vs. Telling
- What and How Questions
- Do vs. Don't,
- Don't!
- Encouragement Circles
- The Two Lists
- Do as I Say
- Taking Care of Yourself
- Think Tree
- Please Be Seated / Cooperative Juggling (together take about 25 minutes)

Activities that can also be taught to students after the teachers practice.

- The Brain in the Palm of the Hand (See *Positive Discipline in the Classroom and School Teachers' Guide: Activities for Students*)
- Charlie (See *Positive Discipline in the Classroom and School Teachers' Guide: Activities for Students*)
- Bugs and Wishes (See *Positive Discipline in the Classroom and School Teachers' Guide: Activities for Students*)
- The Ball of Yarn. A great way to close the school year.

Other short topics that are fun, but also can be a little more challenging and invite more push back:

- Encouragement vs. Praise
- Empowering vs. Enabling
- Competent Giant for Teachers
- Cooperative Juggling for Teachers
- From Laddership to Leadership
- Kindness and Firmness at the Same Time (Grid)
- The Results of Punishment
- The Results of Praise
- Listening: Effective and Ineffective
- Six Approaches to Classroom Discipline
- What Are They Learning?
- The Wright Family
- The Jumbled School House

Asking vs. Telling

From *Positive Discipline Workbook Facilitators'* Guide, Jane Nelsen

Objectives:

- To explore the power of asking instead of telling
- To connect the power of asking to the development of desirable character traits.

Materials:

Sentence strips made from statements below (It is helpful to print the two sets on 2 different colors of paper.)

Character Traits poster from Two Lists Activity.

Comment:

- This activity can be done with one line of volunteers who first read the "A" statements and then read the "B" statements.

Directions:

1. **Set up.**
    - Have two sets of 8 volunteers form two lines (line A and line B) facing each other about 6 feet apart. They will be adults.
    - Distribute statement strips, one to each adult, with the A statements going to one line and the B statements going to the other line.
    - Ask for another volunteer to be a student.
2. **Reading A statements.**
    - Ask the student to stand in front of the first adult in line A, ready to listen as that person reads his/her statement to the student.
    - Ask the student to remain silent, pause and notice what they are thinking, feeling and deciding about the adults and themselves as they hear the words.
    - Have the student proceed down the rest of the line in the same manner, listening to each A statement.
3. **Process.**
    - Ask the student:
        - What are you feeling?
        - What are you thinking or deciding about the adults?
        - What are you thinking or deciding about yourself?
    - Referring to the Character Traits of the Two Lists activity, ask the student which character traits are being developed by the A statements.
4. **Reading B statements**.
    - Have the student stand in front of the first person in line B, ready to listen.
    - Repeat the rest of the steps in #2 and #3 above.
5. **Invite comments** from adults about what they noticed and learned; especially about the character traits they want to develop in students.

Asking vs. Telling Statements

"A" Statements:

1) Listen, you should have your books and homework ready before you come to class!
2) Stop bothering your neighbor!
3) Don't forget to take your coat with you for recess and be sure to put it on...it's cold outside!
4) If you don't get your work done in class you will stay in from recess and get it done then!
5) Stay in your seat!
6) Put your papers away, books back on the shelf and clean up before you leave the classroom!
7) Stop whining and complaining!
8) You shouldn't treat your friends that way.

"B" Statements

1) What do you need to bring with you to be prepared for class?
2) What can you and your classmate do to solve this problem?
3) What do you need to take with you if want to be warm outside at recess?
4) What is your plan for getting your work done before class is over?
5) How does your walking around the room affect your classmates?
6) What do you need to do to clean up your space before you leave this classroom?
7) How can you speak to me so I can hear better what you are saying?
8) What do you think will happen if you continue to treat your friends that way?

Statements for Teachers of Young Children

"A" Statements:

1) Pick up your plate.
2) Push in your chair.
3) Put on your coat.
4) Be quiet.
5) Go lay on your cot.
6) Sit down at the table.
7) Put the toys away.

"B" Statements:

1) Where does your plate belong?
2) What can you do with your chair?
3) What do you need before you can go outside?
4) What kind of voice would help us all hear each other?
5) Remind me of what it is time to do now?
6) What did we agree about eating time?
7) What is your job at clean-up time?

The Ball of Yarn

Lynn Lott and Jane Nelsen

Objective:

- To reflect on the work of the workshop and next steps.
- To recognize the power of each individual to influence and make a difference in their world and the lives of others.
- To understand the power of connection and working together for change.

Materials:

- A ball of yarn.
- Optional: "The Tale of the Hundredth Monkey," (below)

Comment:

- This activity can be done with an imaginary ball of yarn, which has less visual impact, but is also a lot easier to untangle at the end.

Directions:

1. **Form a circle.** Have everyone stand and form a circle.

2. **Set up.** Ask the group to take a moment to reflect and think of:
   - An "aha moment" or something from the workshop that had an impact on you.
   - A personal goal you have set based on what you have learned.

3. **The process for sharing.** Holding the ball of yarn, explain:
   - Each person will have a chance to share.
   - The facilitator will share first and then toss the ball to another person *while keeping hold of the end of the yarn.*
   - The receiving person then shares, tosses the ball to another person again holding onto his or her portion of yarn.
   - The yarn will form a web-like structure.
   - After each person has had a chance to share, the last receiver returns the ball to the facilitator.

4. **Reflection and closure**.
   - Ask participants to pull firm on the yarn so it forms a tight web of connection and think of how our connections support us in the work we do.
   - Remind participants that they are never alone. We are part of a vast network of people both in the community and the world working on behalf of students.
   - Ask them to imagine the students, families and all they will touch in the coming year, actually sitting on this strong web. Remind them that no one of us is responsible for all that happens in education for any one student, but collectively we work for all of the students within our network.
   - Ask them to imagine that each of the people they impact in turn has his or her own circle of influence and the skills learned continually spread outward.

5. **Optional.** Share the "Tale of the Hundredth Monkey," or talk for a minute about how rapidly access to the Internet has spread around the world (the first conceptualizations for the Internet date from the early 1960s).

6. **Closure:** Ask participants to pause, take a final look at the web and carefully place the yarn on the floor. Ask for a volunteer to roll up the yarn.

The Tale of the Hundredth Monkey*

On an island somewhere in the vast ocean there was a colony of monkeys who ate dirty sweet potatoes. One day, one monkey decided to wash his sweet potato in the ocean. Another monkey watched with curiosity and then decided to wash his sweet potato in the ocean. The adage, "monkey see, monkey do" proved to be true as each monkey who saw another monkey wash his sweet potato soon copied this wonderful idea.

As the story goes, when the hundredth monkey on this island washed her sweet potato in the ocean, suddenly all the other monkeys on all the neighboring islands started to wash their sweet potatoes even though they had not seen it done by other monkeys.

The moral of the story: it takes only one person (or monkey) to start something wonderful. When enough others join in this practice, a consciousness is created that spreads throughout the world.

We have now created a small network of people who are committed to treating children with dignity and respect. Together we can create a consciousness that will eventually spread throughout the world.

* Based upon The Tale of the Hundredth Monkey, A Story About Social Change, by Ken Keyes. Read more about this story at: http://www.wowzone.com/monkey.htm, including this concluding statement from researcher, Elaine Meyers:

"What the research does suggest... is that holding positive ideas (as important a step as this is) is not sufficient by itself to change the world. We still need direct communication between individuals, we need to translate our ideas into action, and we need to recognize the freedom of choice of those who choose alternatives different from our own."

Competent Giant for Teachers

Adapted from an activity Virginia Satir, published by John Taylor[6]

Objective:	**Directions**:
• To explore the impact of negative comments and reprimands on students and their behaviors. • To explore the results of decisions made by students in response to adult actions. **Materials:** • The list of challenges from the "Two Lists" activity • Flip Chart Paper • Markers **Comments:** • This activity presumes that participants have previously done the Two Lists and Brain in the Palm of the Hand activities. • Negative comments/ reprimanding can momentarily stop misbehavior. • The long-term results of negative comments/ reprimands include: rupture of relationships and students making negative decisions about themselves, adults and school.	**1. Getting started.** • Ask participants what kind of things they have heard other teachers say or do when their buttons have been pushed and/or when they have flipped their lid. • Scribe these statements/actions on a flip chart. **2. Divide into pairs.** • Ask participants to divide into pairs. • One person, role-playing the adult, will stand on a chair. The other person, role-playing the student, will stand on the floor in front of the adult. (If standing on the chairs does not work for the group, have adults stand on the floor and "students" kneel directly in front of them) **3. Role-play.** • Have the adult imagine that the student is doing a behavior from the Challenges List that *really* pushes their buttons. Imagine that the student has repeatedly done that behavior, and the adult has flipped his/her lid. • Have the adult chose one of the humiliating statements just brainstormed by the group, or one of their own, and deliver it to the student standing or kneeling below him/her. **4. Switch roles.** • After about 30 seconds of role-playing, ask participants to switch roles so they experience both positions. **5. Process with the adults.** • Ask participants to share what they were thinking, feeling, and deciding when role-playing the adult. • If it hasn't come out, ask, "How many of you found it difficult to role-play being 'flipped' and making these statements?" • Ask, "How many of you have noticed that when you hear someone else treat a student like this it sounds so terrible, but when you are doing it, it is because the student deserves it?" • Ask, "What is the intention of teachers when they scold or say humiliating things to a student?" If their answer does not include "desire to help the student behave

[6] *Person to Person: Awareness Techniques for Counselors, Group Leaders, and Parent Educators* John Taylor 1984, RE Publishers, Saratoga, California.

	better" mention it yourself. **6. Process with the students.** • Jokingly ask, "How many of you, while looking up at the nostrils of the adult in front of you, were thinking, 'This teacher is so helpful. I appreciate this feedback so much. I can hardly wait to bring all my problems to this very encouraging teacher?'" • Ask students to share what they were really thinking, feeling, and deciding about the adult. • Ask students to share what they were thinking, feeling, and deciding about themselves. • How might these decisions impact your behavior and/or what you do in the future? **7. Reflection.** • Ask participants what they learned from this activity. • As adults we often revert to this behavior because it's what was modeled for us. • When we flip our lids, we temporarily lose the functions of our prefrontal cortex, and can feel angry, self-righteous and/or justified in our actions. When our prefrontal cortex re-engages, we often feel guilty or remorseful. **8. Moving it forward.** This activity leads to deep and rich discussions. It can be taken in many directions when followed by other activities. Such as: • **Repair.** The *3 R's of Recovery* helps teachers with the skills to rebuild relationships. • **Exploring the student's world.** The *What and How Questions* activity offers a solution-focused alternative. • **Getting support and encouragement.** The *Encouragement Circles* activity helps teachers recognize that they are less likely to flip their lid in a community of support. • **Understanding the Belief Behind the Behavior.** Any mistaken goal activity can help teachers understand that misbehavior is a misguided attempt to get belonging and significance. • **Impacts of decisions.** The *Results of Punishment* activity digs deeper into the kinds of decisions we make when we perceive we have been punished.

Continuum of Change

Origins of the Conscious Competence Model are not known (See link below)

Objective:

- To recognize change as a process involving awareness and skill development.
- To become more aware of how each individual works through the process of change at their own pace and in their own way.

Materials:

Prepared flip chart sheet divided into 4 vertical columns as shown below

Comments:

- Once we recognize that change is a process instead of an event, we can be more encouraging and compassionate with ourselves and others as we learn.
- This activity is extremely helpful and can be used at different times in a workshop; this will impact the processing. See #8.
- In some communities learning to ride a bike is not a commonly shared experience. It is helpful (but not always possible) to brainstorm to find an experience that engages the body as well as the mind.

Directions:

1. **Set up.** Invite participants to remember their experience of learning to ride a bike.
2. **Observing.**
   - Invite participants to remember a time when they were young, watching other kids have fun riding their bikes.
   - Ask, "At that moment, what were you feeling or thinking watching them ride?" Note that some people are happy where they are.
   - *Leaving the top header blank*, write their feelings and thoughts in the first column.
3. **First attempts.**
   - Invite participants to remember what it was like to get on the bike and try to ride for the first time (maybe with help from an adult or training wheels).
   - *Leaving the top header blank,* write their feelings and thoughts in the second column.
4. **Practicing.**
   - Invite participants to remember when they could ride….sort of….but it was still challenging around corners, up hills or stopping.
   - *Leaving the top header blank*, write their feelings and thoughts in the third column.
5. **Mastering the skill**.
   - Invite participants to remember when they were skilled enough to ride down hills, around corners, or ride with no hands etc.
   - *Leaving the header blank*, write feelings and thought in the fourth column.
6. **Label the columns.**

   Put the appropriate heading at the top of each column.
   - Column 1. Unconsciously Unskilled
   - Column 2. Consciously Unskilled
   - Column 3. Consciously Skilled
   - Column 4. Unconsciously Skilled
7. **Process.**

   Ask participants:
   - What did you notice?
   - How does this apply to your daily life?
   - What happens when you are exposed to a new concept even within your field of expertise?
   - When are you most able to take on new challenges?

Remind participants that once we learn to ride a bike, the skill

	is mastered. However, when we are using skills that involve people, our emotional "buttons" may get pushed and the learned skill may temporarily seem to disappear. **8. Continue processing.** Additional processing will change depending on the timing of this activity. The discussion can be brought forward with the following considerations. *Activity used at the beginning or alone* • To enhance awareness and introduce the process of change. *Activity used in the middle of a workshop* • To invite compassion for the challenging feelings that come with being consciously unskilled and the work of being consciously skilled. *Activity used in the end of a workshop* • To warn participants that they have made big changes and may be eager to share with others. The people with whom they would like to share begin as unconsciously unskilled. Suggestions move the listener to the uncomfortable feelings associated with becoming consciously unskilled. Those feelings are not usually welcomed and may result in resistance or finding fault with the new tools. • It is best to model and answer questions when asked than to tell or teach your exciting new tools to those you love and care about.

Sample of finished chart: *The top row is left blank until Step 6.*

Unconsciously Unskilled	Consciously Unskilled	Consciously Skilled	Unconsciously Skilled
Fun Easy Freedom Indifferent Oblivious Longing to be part of the group Those are the big guys. A little scary Where I am is fine	Scared Hurt Challenged Exciting Wobbly Uncertain Discouraged	Lonely Excited Scared Nervous Hard work Frustrated Discouraged Proud Determined Hyper alert	Easy Freedom Proud Successful Ready to take on new challenge Forget how hard it was. Part of the group

For more information on this model see:
http://www.businessballs.com/consciouscompetencelearningmodel.htm

Cooperative Juggling for Teachers

Adapted from *Positive Discipline in the Classroom Teacher's Guide,* Jane Nelsen and Lynn Lott.

Objective:

- To understand the power of routines.
- To highlight how easily routines get derailed.
- To understand the need for students to anticipate and practice recovering their routines in unusual or stressful situations.

Materials:

- 5-7 Koosh balls or soft bean bags.
- A small plastic wrench (preferred) or any other highly unusual object (rubber chicken).

Comments:

- Well-established routines are one of three pillars of effective classroom leadership. (Agreements, Routines, Meaningful Work)
- Well-established routines are often disrupted by unexpected events.
- When students practice the routines with imaginary disruptions their skill level in handling daily disruptions improves.

Directions:

1. **Setting up the juggling.**
    - Ask for 6 - 8 volunteers to practice group juggling with you.
    - Together, stand and form a circle.
    - Ask others in the room to be observers.
2. **Juggling Round 1.**
    - Tell your volunteers that their goal in juggling is to keep the balls in the air and not to let them hit the ground.
    - Quickly start tossing the balls in the air in the general direction of the volunteers in the circle.
    - After a few moments of chaos, tell everyone to freeze.
3. **Pause, reflect and make a plan.**
    - Ask, "What is going on?" (Chaos!)
    - "What could we do to make this work better?"
    - Invite the group to offer suggestions. These will include things like: make a pattern, making eye contact and calling someone's name before a ball is gently thrown. If they don't suggest creating a pattern, it is important to suggest it.
    - Review the group's ideas (including yours if it is needed), e.g., "What I heard was that you want to try to make a pattern, make eye contact, and throw gently."
    - Ask the volunteers to return the balls to you.
4. **Juggling Round 2.**
    - Ask the group if they would be willing try incorporating the suggestions by starting with just one ball to establish a pattern and get practice.
    - Ask them to make sure that each volunteer only gets the ball once. (One easy way to do this is to direct them to hold their hands out if they have NOT had the ball, and to put them down once they have received it.)
    - Start by throwing the ball to one volunteer.
    - Finish the pattern by having the last volunteer throw the ball back to you.
    - Check to make sure everyone can remember who they got the ball from and to whom they threw the ball.
    - Ask if they want to practice one more time with just one ball. (Follow their decision.)
    - Begin "juggling" again using the pattern and other guidelines, adding balls so that the whole circle is active again.

5. Pause and reflect.
- How did we do?
- Observers, what did you notice?
- What did we learn from this process?
- How many of us did it take to be successful?
- What happened after we took time to practice?
- What did it take for us to get better at working together?
- How could we apply this to our school/classroom?
- Is there anything we could do to make our juggling better?

6. Juggling Round 3.
- Ask the group if they would be willing to juggle together one more time to see if we can do it even better and see if it could go even faster.
- Start throwing the balls.
- Shortly into the process, without breaking the pattern or saying anything, introduce the wrench or chosen object in place of a ball.
- Then continue and complete the process using the remaining balls.

7. Pause and reflect.
- What happened in this round?
- How did it impact our process?
- How does even a slight change impact school or classroom routines?
- Can we prevent unexpected change?
- How did working together and practicing the process help prepare us for the unexpected change?
- What would improve our response to surprises like this?
- How might that apply to the classroom?

8. Moving it forward. Brainstorm ways to help students practice routines in the face of unexpected events. Students enjoy representing the disruption in role-play.
Examples:
- Practice lining up in a hurry because the teacher lost track of time.
- Practice getting back on task after someone has come in the room for an important announcement.
- Practice returning to task after a fire drill.
- Practice staying on task when an observer wanders through the classroom.

Do As I Say

Ruben Castaneda

<table>
<tr>
<td>

Objective:
To demonstrate to teachers how some students' actions are based on behavior learned from adults around them.

To introduce mirror neurons.

Materials: None

Comment:
This is a lovely set-up for understanding the power of modeling and mirror neurons.

</td>
<td>

Directions:
1. Gather the group's attention. Model and ask the group:
<ul>
<li>To put their eyes on you.</li>
<li>To put both feet flat on the floor (you may be standing, but they will probably be sitting).</li>
<li>To place both hands on their knees and to take a deep breath and exhale.</li>
</ul>
2. Begin and model intentional action. Ask the group to make a circle with their index finger and thumb as if signing "okay."

3. Continue action with words that do not match. Do this with confidence as if nothing is abnormal.
<ul>
<li>State, "Now place the circle on your chin", while at the same time you place *your circle on your cheek.*</li>
<li>Observe the group: most of them will have followed what you *did.* Watch for those who catch themselves and try to adjust.</li>
</ul>
4. Reflection. Keeping your hand on your cheek, ask the group,
<ul>
<li>Where did you put your hand? (Many will have followed your actions, not your words.)</li>
<li>Why did that happen?</li>
<li>Why do you have it on your cheek?</li>
<li>What are we learning in terms of teaching/modeling for children?</li>
<li>What are some behaviors they may have noticed their student picked up from them?</li>
<li>What do they need to do if they expect a different behavior from their student in the future?</li>
</ul>
Extension:
Introduce mirror neurons. If you don't know much about mirror neurons watch http://video.pbs.org/video/1615173073/
<ul>
<li>We are hardwired to learn by watching.</li>
<li>When watching an intentional action, our brain gets ready to do the same thing.</li>
<li>This is present from birth. (When you stick your tongue out to an alert newborn 3 times, the baby will copy you. When you see someone yawn, you may find yourself repressing your own yawn.)</li>
<li>Mirror neurons work for emotions too. By engaging the emotional parts of our brain through our mirror neurons we are actually able feel other people's emotions. It is part of our brain's natural empathy system.</li>
</ul>

</td>
</tr>
</table>

Do vs. Don't

Kelly Pfeiffer

<table>
<tr>
<td>

Objective:

- Understanding the power of telling students what *to do* instead of what *not* to do.
- The language we use has profound impacts.

Materials:
Flip chart, markers
Cue cards for your instructions (below)

Comments:
This activity stands alone or can be used to complement and enhance other practices.

- Punishment focuses on what not to do instead of what to do.
- Routines help students know what to do.
- The Wheel of Choice offers ideas for what to do.
- Bugs and Wishes teaches students to ask for what they want (helping the other student know what to do.)

</td>
<td>

Directions:

1. Introduce activity.

- Ask participants to simply follow the instructions.
- There will be two rounds.

2. Round 1.

- Give the commands/instructions pausing briefly after each.
- After all of the instructions, say, "That was the end of round 1. Now we will do round 2."

3. Round 2. Give the commands for round two.

4. Reflection.

- Ask participants "What was different between round 1 and round 2?"
- Record responses which will look like:
  Round 1: Harder, required more thinking, I wasn't sure what to do, confusing, slower
  Round 2: Easier, I knew what to do, faster, clear, simple to process.
- What did you learn from this about instructions?

5. Moving it forward.

- On a separate sheet, again divided into two columns. Title the left column "Don't" and the right, "Do."
- Ask participants to share things for which they hear themselves and others saying, "Don't" (Scribe in left column.) Eg. Don't hit, Don't run, Don't yell, etc.
- Invite the group to brainstorm "Do" statements that correspond to each "Don't" statement.
- What did you learn/notice from this?

Modifications:
Use this activity with the Don't activity.

</td>
</tr>
</table>

Cue cards for your instructions:

Statements for Round 1:
Don't sit down
Don't put your hands by your sides
Don't close your mouth
Don't open your mouth
Don't look at me
Don't stand still
Don't stand up

Statements for Round 2:
Stand up
Raise your hands
Open your mouth
Close your mouth
Look at another person
Walk around the room
Sit down

Don't!

Bill Scott

Objective:	Directions:
• To recognize the power of the words we use because of images they create in the minds of the listeners. • The images created by a "don't" statement invite the opposite of what we want. **Materials:** • Wipe-off board or chart paper • Markers **Comments:** • When giving directions or instructions our words should create the image of what we want. • Helping students develop pictures of appropriate behavior invites appropriate action. • This activity works well with "Do vs. Don't"	**1. Give command statements.** • Ask participants to close their eyes and listen • Speaking with authority, say, - "Don't hit your friend!" - "Don't put your book on the floor!" - "Don't run in the hall!" - "Don't think of a pink elephant!" • Have participants open their eyes. **2. Process.** • Ask participants what they "saw" in their heads when you said, "Don't think of a pink elephant!" • What did they envision for the other statements? • Participants will typically say, "A pink elephant," "A book on the floor," and "A child running down the hall." • When we need to correct student behavior, do we want them to "picture" the misbehavior, or the correct behavior? **3. Practice.** • Divide the chart into two columns. • Brainstorm a few typical "don't" statements that are likely to be said by adults in a school and write them in the left column • Brainstorm alternative statements that would likely create mental images of a student behaving in a more appropriate way and write them in the right column.

Encouragement Circles

Based upon "Circle of Love" from *Positive Discipline for Single Parents Facilitator's Guide,* by Jane Nelsen and Cheryl Erwin. Revised by Jody McVittie

<table>
<tr>
<td>

Objective:
To enhance awareness of the power of and need for encouragement for the adults in the school community.

Materials:
Flip Chart
Markers

Comments:
There are two reasons the directions indicate that the encourager should give a statement that he/she would like to hear.

- It removes the responsibility of finding the "right" comment.
- Personally speaking the statement is also a form of self-encouragement.

</td>
<td>

Directions:

1. **Preparing the group.** As a group, brainstorm things that would be helpful/encouraging to hear after having a stressful day. Scribe them on the flip chart. Examples might include:
    - I'm glad you are my co-worker.
    - I saw you working with [student's name] today and it made a difference.
    - You make a difference.
    - I can tell you've had a tough day.
    - When I watch you work with your students I can tell you really care about them.
    - I appreciate the effort you have put in today.
    - Etc.
2. **Set up the circle.**
    - Count the number of people in the room and make a circle of chairs that face the center. Use ½ the number of chairs as there are people.
    - Invite ½ of the people to sit in the chairs.
    - The other participants each stand behind a seated person.
3. **Sharing encouragement, round 1.**
    - The standing participants whisper one of the encouraging statements that they personally would like to hear to the person in front of them (not what they think the person would like to hear).
    - Then everyone rotate to the right.
    - Repeat this process about 5-10 times (This process can be very encouraging. Consider completing the circle if time permits.)
4. **Sharing encouragement, round 2.** Have the participants switch places. Repeat step 3.
5. **Reflection.** When both sets of participants have received and given, invite them to go back to the larger circle and process.
    - What did you notice?
    - How did it feel to give encouragement?
    - How did it feel to receive encouragement?
    - Anything else?
6. **Moving it forward.** Invite a discussion about how what they learned here might be used in a school to encourage each other. School staff long for encouragement.

</td>
</tr>
</table>

Empowering vs. Enabling

Jane Nelsen and Lynn Lott

<table>
<tr>
<td>

Objectives:

- To learn the concept and skills of empowering young people.
- To explore our use of firmness.

Materials:

- Strips of paper with empowering statements, and strips with enabling statements.
- "Helpful Hints for Empowering vs. Enabling" handout for each participant

Comments:

- We do not necessarily feel comfortable with empowering statements and actions until we really understand the long-range benefits.
- Seeing punishment as a form of enabling is a shift in perspective.

</td>
<td>

Directions:

1. **Brief introduction:** We are going to step into exploring firmness from a few different angles.
2. **Setting up the activity.**
   - Ask for a volunteer to role-play the part of a student who has not been doing his/her homework.
   - Ask for volunteers to role-play the part of teachers and form two lines each of 8- 10 people facing each other about 8 feet apart.
   - Give one group of teachers the slips for empowering statements, and the other group the enabling statements.
   - The "student" will go back and forth between the two lines. In front of each "teacher" the student will say, "I haven't done my homework." The "teacher" reads his/her response and the "student" listens before going on to the next teacher.
3. **Reflection and processing with the student.** Ask:
   - What were you feeling?
   - What decisions were you making about the adults in your life?
   - What decisions were you making about yourself?
   - What were you deciding to do?"
   - (Optional: Which group did he/she sensed cared more. Which group did he/she respect more?)
4. **Reflection and processing with each line of the teachers.** Ask
   - How were you feeling?
   - What decisions were you making about the student?
   - What decisions were you making about yourself?"
5. **Reflection and process with the group.**
   - What did you learn?
6. **Enabling vs. Empowering**.
   - Hand out "Helpful Hints for Empowering vs. Enabling."
   - Read the definitions.
   - Invite comments. (Keep them limited.)

Extension/modification:

- It can be useful to give the "student" a set of objects (bean bags in a larger bag, a stack of cups) after they have gone back and forth once or twice and add an extra instruction. "Imagine that this bag/cup is responsibility. When you say, "I haven't done my homework" pass the "responsibility (bag/cup)" to the "teacher." Listen to sense whether he/she kept the responsibility or whether he/she gave it back. Either leave the object with the teacher or take it back depending on where you think the responsibility lies.

</td>
</tr>
</table>

Helpful Hints for Empowering vs. Enabling Handout

Jane Nelsen and Lynn Lott, adapted by Jody McVittie

We have become vividly aware of how skilled most of us are in enabling responses and how unskilled we are in empowering responses.

Our definition of *enabling* is: "Getting between young people and life experiences to minimize the consequences of their choices." Enabling responses include:

- Doing too much for them
- Giving them too much
- Overprotecting/rescuing
- Lying for them
- Punishing/controlling
- Living in denial
- Fixing
- Bailing them out

Our definition of *empowering* is: "Turning control over to young people as soon as possible so they have power over their own lives." Empowering responses include:

- Listening and giving emotional support and validation without fixing or discounting
- Teaching life skills
- Working on agreements through class meetings or the joint problem-solving process
- Letting go (without abandoning)
- Deciding what *you* will do with dignity and respect
- Sharing what you think, how you feel, and what you want (without lecturing, moralizing, insisting on agreement, or demanding that anyone give you what you want)
- Sticking to the issue with dignity and respect

More hints:

- Enabling responses tend to be easier for most of us than empowering responses. The statements below may seem awkward.
- Punishment is enabling, not because of the lack of firmness, but because
  - Control remains with the adult.
  - The focus moves from the problem to a power/revenge relationship between the adult and child.
  - The young person often believes he/she has "made the payment" and therefore can drop the problem.
  - The young person and adult can shift their focus to resentment instead of problem solving.
  - The young person no longer takes responsibility for finding a solution.

Enabling/Empowering Statements

Enabling Statements

"Well then, you fail. I'll call your parents about this."

"I can't believe you have procrastinated again. What will ever become of you? You can turn it in tomorrow this time, but next time you'll just have to suffer the consequences."

"You can have a prize from my treasure box if you finish your work by lunch time."

"Bless your heart. I know that work was too hard for you. I should have never given it to you. Let's get Ms. Jones to help you with it."

"You are having a tough week. It's okay with me if you just finish the first page."

"Well, sweetie, I'm sure you don't really need to do all your assignments. You are smart enough to do just fine without some of them."

"How many times have I told you to pay attention and get your work done? Why can't you be more like your brother? Why can't you be more responsible? What will become of you?"

"How come you always forget and never get your work done? I can't believe you are so lazy."

"I thought you would do your work after I was so kind to you and let you be my helper and take that message to all the other teachers in the building. You are so disappointing."

"Well, no wonder! I saw you wasting your time, looking out the window. You should feel ashamed of yourself. You'd better shape up or you'll be shipping out to live on the streets like a bum."

"I've had it. You had plenty of warning. You can't go on the field trip."

"I just don't understand. I excused you from finishing your work over and over, every time you have asked, and it doesn't seem to help at all!"

Empowering Statements

EXPRESSING YOUR LIMITS: "I'm available to help with homework before school on Tuesdays and Thursdays. I won't be available to help with last-minute projects."

EXPRESSING YOUR LIMITS: "I'm willing to give you extra time in the library when we come to an agreement in advance for a convenient time, but I'm not willing to get involved at the last minute."

LOVING AND ENCOURAGING: "Do you know that I care about you no matter what – and that you are more important to me than your grades?"

JOINT PROBLEM SOLVING: "What is your picture of what is going on regarding your work? Would you be willing to hear my concerns? Could we brainstorm together on some possible solutions?"

CONNECT FIRST: "I can see that you feel bad about getting that poor grade. I have faith in you to learn from this and figure out what you need to do to get the grade you would like."

LETTING GO OF THEIR ISSUES: "I feel upset when you don't do your work because I value education so much. I think a good education could be very beneficial to you in your life. I really wish you would do your work."

AGREEMENT, NOT RULES: "Could we sit down and see if we can work on a plan regarding class work that we both can live with?"

LISTEN WITHOUT FIXING OR JUDGING: "I would like to hear what this means for you. Can you explain to me why it isn't important to you to do your assignments?"

SHOWING FAITH: "I have faith in you. I trust you to figure out what you need. I know that when it is important to you, you'll know what to do."

CURIOSITY: What is your plan?

CURIOSITY: What is your picture of what is going on regarding your homework?

Empowering/Enabling Statements for Younger Children

Jody McVittie, Steven Foster and Laurie Prusso Hatch

One way to set this up is to have the adults in two lines. Have "child" sit on the floor and have the adults walk by him/her –one set (enablers/empowerers) of adults passing on the right, the other set on the left stopping to address the issue with the child.

Enabling statements:

It is clean-up time. Why are you just sitting there?

You act like this every day? Is there something wrong with you?

All of your friends are able to help. I wonder if you are just a baby, not a big girl?

Pick up the toys now, or you will sit on the chair instead of joining us at Circle.

I am going to set the timer for 3 minutes and these better be picked up.

We go through this every day! I am tired of it.

If you want to play with these again, you'd better get them picked up right now!

It's okay; Jacob can do it for you.

Here, I'll do it with you (and essentially do it for child).

You can come back and pick them up later.

Empowering Statements:

Show faith with a reminder of what the student can do. "I have seen you carry really heavy things before. I know you can do it."

Respond with a question. "I wonder how many ways you can figure out how to do this?"

Acknowledge feelings. "You were really having fun here. It is hard to stop playing to clean up. Which blocks do you want to put on the shelf first?"

Check the child's knowledge or understanding. "What is supposed to be happening now?"

Invite cooperation. "I know you like to be a helper. Do you want to do it and sing at the same time?"

Limited choices. "Do you want to put the big blocks away first or the small blocks?"

Say what you want/mean. Get down at the child's level and with a smile, calmly say, "[name], it is time to put the blocks away now."

Use non-verbal language. Put a gentle hand on his or her shoulder. Look at him/her in the eye (pause to notice the feeling) and with friendly eyes indicate what needs to happen.

Connect and redirect. "It looks like you were enjoying your play and you don't want to stop. How about I pick up the squares and you pick up the rectangles?"

Look for other solutions. "I wonder if one of your friends would come and help you. Who could you ask?"

Connect and redirect. "It is always more fun if we work together. What would you like me to do to help?" (With caution to not do "for")

Encouragement vs. Praise

Mickie Berry

<table>
<tr>
<td>

Objective:
To help people understand the difference between encouragement and praise and the long-range effects of each.

Materials:
Sticky notes or 8 x 11 sheets with statements

Comments:
- We can never be sure what kids are deciding, but we can do things that are more likely to invite healthy decisions.
- Praise, like candy, can be enjoyable once in awhile. Encouragement, however, should be the staple that you give to yourself and your students every day.
- Encouragement allows students to see themselves as being capable, and values their effort rather than focusing on perfection or pleasing others.

</td>
<td>

Directions:

1. **Preparation.** Have ready 10-12 praise statements and 10-12 encouragement statements on 2x2 sticky notes or on 8X11 sheets. (See below).
2. **Set up the activity.**
   - Ask for two volunteers to come up and pretend that they are students and listen to statements.
   - Ask the audience to listen as if they were students as well.
3. **Give praise.** Give the praise statements to the first student as you hand him/her the sheets or put the sticky notes on his/her shirt.
4. **Give encouragement.** Give the encouragement statements to the other student as above.
5. **Process/reflection with the "students."** Ask the "students"
   - What were they feeling?
   - What were they deciding?
   - Did they like one set of statements better? Would one of them like to trade? (No right answer here).
6. **Process/reflection with the group.**
   - What did they notice?
   - What did they learn?
   - If it hasn't come out yet, make the distinction between encouragement and praise.
   - If it has not come out in the processing, ask the group to think about how a person who had received mostly praise all his/her life would know when he/she was doing a good job as an adult. (Would need someone to tell him/her?) How would someone receiving encouragement know? (Would have an internal sense.)

</td>
</tr>
</table>

Extension/modifications:
- Use two rows of teachers giving first praise and then encouragement statements.
- Use 3 people, ignoring the person in the middle. We can discourage students without doing anything intentional.
- Often teachers feel less skilled at encouragement and want "the list" of statements. The following extension helps them recognize how easy it is to encourage.
- Partner practice: Ask participants to find a practice partner and lead the following: (next page)

Round 1. Descriptive encouragement.
Ask participants to each give their partner two descriptive encouragement statements. Descriptive encouragement often starts with "I notice…." and is not necessarily "positive." Offer examples: I notice you seem upset today, I notice you are in a hurry, I noticed how delighted you were with your project.

Round 2. Appreciative encouragement.
Ask participants to each give their partner two appreciative encouragement statements. Appreciative encouragement often starts with "I appreciate…" or "Thank you for…." Examples include: I appreciated your help. Thank you for pausing and walking. I appreciate how much work you've put into this. *Notice that there are no value judgment words like "good" "well" "best."*

Round 3. Empowering Encouragement. (This is the hardest)
Ask participants to each give their partner one empowering encouragement statement. Empowering encouragement often starts with "I trust you to…" "I know you…." "I have faith…" Examples include: "I trust you to figure this one out." "I have faith that you'll be able to solve this." *Note, that for older students and students exposed to trauma you will need to show your "evidence" so that your judgment feels authentic.* An example might be, "I saw how persistent you can be when you are shooting hoops. It will only take half of that kind of persistence for you to be able to get this done. I know you can do it."

Praise and Encouragement Statements

(Pick about 10 of each)

Praise

I'm proud of you

You are so smart!
Your painting/project is beautiful.
I wish other kids could do it like you.*
Good job.
Good boy/girl.
You did it just like I told you.
You're the best player on your team.

You always know the right answer.
I like how you stood up for yourself
You outshined all those other kids.

You got an A again. I'm expecting you to keep it up.
You know just how to please me 100%
I'm impressed.
Great! That's what I expected!
I like it.

Encouragement

Look what you accomplished! You could feel proud about that.
Look how much you've learned since 2 months ago.
Can you tell me about your painting/project?
I can tell you worked hard on this.
I care about you.
Thanks for your cooperation. It helped me out.
Thank you for your help. It made my day easier.
Are you noticing how much you've helped your team?
You figured it out.
It took courage to stand up for yourself like that.
What was most important to you about what you learned?
Have you noticed? You reached your goal!

I have faith in you.
Look how far you've come.
You really stuck it out and you accomplished what you wanted.
You can decide that for yourself. I trust you to make the decision that is right for you.
I trust your judgment, Go for it.

* We don't always say "I wish other students could do it like you," however we do say things like "Look how Jason is sitting" or "Monique has her papers out and is ready to start" and thereby put one student above the others in attempt to get other students to comply.

From Laddership to Leadership

Activity based on the work of Steve Maybell
Jody McVittie and Lois Ingber

Objective:	**Directions:**
• To explore the implications of vertical relationships. • To recognize skills necessary for effective leadership in a democratic community. • To recognize the importance of shared visions/agreements. **Materials:** • Flip chart and markers. Sample chart below for reference. • Optional: toy ladder **Comments:** • As democratic relationships become more prevalent in schools, families and organizations, the tools needed for effective leadership change. • The time of transition toward a more horizontal or democratic system can be messy. • The process of developing a shared vision/goal is one of many leadership challenges in this paradigm.	1. **Set up.** • Explain briefly: In the past it was normal and acceptable to have people with superior positions and people with inferior positions. • Illustrate this by naming some examples. Using only the top half of the flip chart, write the "superior" position on the top, and the "inferior" position at the bottom underneath its corresponding superior position. (Leaving most of the flip chart blank in between) • List the following pairs: kings/ peasants, boss /workers, teachers/students, adults /children, men/women, light skinned/dark skinned. See sample below. 2. **Identify the tools of power.** Pointing to the row of people on the top ask how these people maintained their position above the people below them. • What tools did they use? See sample below. • Scribe the answers in the space between the two groups of people. 3. **The impact of vertical relationships.** Let the group know that we call these "vertical relationships." Ask: • What do you think the people on the bottom might be feeling, thinking or deciding about the people on the top? • What are the people on the bottom feeling, thinking or deciding about themselves? 4. **Change is happening.** People on the bottom have decided they want and deserve to be treated with equal dignity and respect. When they have a sense of worthiness, how effective are the old tools? 5. **Horizontal relationships.** • Draw a horizontal line across the bottom half of the paper. • Ask, "What kinds of tools are needed for people to work together effectively? (Participants will list things like cooperation, respect, responsibility, communication, celebrate differences, collaboration etc). Record these near the line. • Ask, "Where do we learn those tools?" • Why does it seem so messy? The idea that comes out here is that power tools are familiar and part of our language. We are less skilled at the cooperation tools; they often take longer and need to be revised during

<table>
<tr>
<td></td>
<td>
the change process.

6. The importance of a common vision.
• If they happen to identify some kind of common vision, goal or set of agreements, change the line to an arrow facing right and write shared vision/goal at the end of the arrow.
• If they do not mention a common goal/vision/agreements ask, “How will people know where they are going?”
• Once the words “vision” or “goals” or “agreements” are on the chart, remind them that the leader in this paradigm has a different role. He /she did not set the goals alone – it is done collaboratively.
• Instead of making the group reach the goals, the leader becomes the steward for the shared vision. He/she can then lead from anywhere in the group – not always out front.
• What does this tell us about the importance of classroom/school agreements? Refer to the section on making agreements in Positive Discipline in the Classroom and School Teachers' Guide: Activities for Students.

7. Reflection/Summary.
• You can look at this as a change from Laddership (top down) to Leadership (horizontal).
• Horizontal relationships don't mean that everyone is the same or has the same responsibilities but do mean everyone is treated with dignity and respect.
• Administrators, teachers and parents have clear leadership roles with distinct responsibilities.
</td>
</tr>
</table>

Sample Completed Laddership to Leadership Chart:

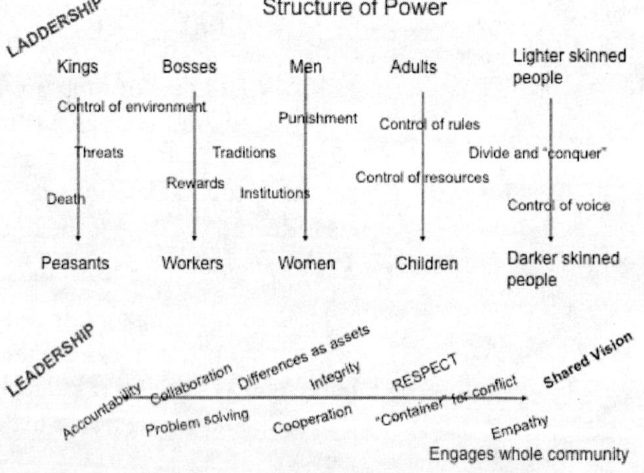

The Jumbled Schoolhouse Activity

Suzanne Smitha
Based upon work from Rutgers University
Collaborative for Academic, Social and Emotional Learning (CASEL)

Objective:

- To provide a visual representation promoting Social-Emotional and Character Development skills as the framework that pulls a school together.
- To provide a brief reference to recent research relating social-emotional skills and character development to academic learning and success in life.
- To establish that such a framework can provide criteria against which a school evaluates new processes or program options.

Materials:

- Enlarged and cut-out pieces of Jumbled Schoolhouse available at www.positivediscipline.org go to Jumbled School House under Free Resources and Links to retrieve copy or the power point version of the jumbled schoolhouse.
- Fabric sticky sheet (see directions below), felt board or power point equipment.

Comments:

- If you want a deeper

Directions:

1. **Introduce Jumbled House.**
   Show the pieces of the schoolhouse.
   - If using fabric or felt board scatter the pieces of the school house on the lower half of your fabric/board.
   - If using a power point, show the slide with the scattered pieces.
   - Describe this as a school without a common framework.
   - Without a guiding framework against which a school evaluates new programs or processes, the school's efforts, over time, will be uncoordinated and will lack efficiency, organization, coherence and direction.
   - As a result, student progress will be impacted.
2. **Explain the importance of educating the whole child with both an academic and social-emotional/character education framework.**
   - Children need to develop academic and critical thinking skills to equip them for success in life.
   - Children also need effective relational skills, including respect for self and others, ability to problem solve, good character, and a sense of their capability to contribute to the greater good of the community.
   - Among the top 11 most influential factors impacting student learning, 8 involve social-emotional learning, student/teacher interaction, classroom climate and peer group. (Wang, 1997)[8]
   - "When a whole school intentionally addresses culture, climate and social and emotional curriculum, test scores improve 11 percentile points." (Weissberg & Durlak, 2011)[9]
3. **Share the components of an effective social-emotional/character education program (Elias, 2006)[10].**
   - *Knowing self and others:* identifying feelings, being responsible, recognizing strengths.
   - *Making responsible decisions:* managing emotions,

---

[8] Wang, M. C., Haertel, G. D., & Walberg, H. J. (1997).Toward a knowledge base for school learning. Review of Education Research, 63, 249-294.

[9] Weissberg, Roger P., and Durlak, Joseph A. (2011) The impact of enhancing students' social and emotional learning: A meta-analysis of school-based universal interventions. Retrieved from http://casel.org/why-it-matters/benefits-of-sel/meta-analysis. Full text retrieved from: http://onlinelibrary.wiley.com

[10] Elias ,Maurice J. (2006). The connection between academic and social emotional learning in *The Educator's Guide to Emotional Intelligence and Academic Achievement*, by Maurice J. Elias and Harriett Arnold. Thousand Oaks, CA: Corwin Press,

knowledge base before doing this activity, read the page in the Theory section of this manual and/or the links provided. • There is extensive research on Social Emotional Learning and how it impacts students, learning and the culture of schools[7]. • Permission to print, enlarge, or convert the image below to PowerPoint is granted from Dr. Elias for use with this activity. • When presenting the activity credit should clearly be given to Dr. Elias and the DSACS Team. Elias, Maurice J. and the DSACS_SECD Team (www.teachSECD.com). Guidelines for putting the pieces together: How to go from the jumbled schoolhouse to the synergized schoolhouse. Retrieved from www.docstoc.com/docs/91651933	solving problems creatively, setting goals and planning, understanding situations. • *Caring for others:* showing empathy, respect for self and others, appreciation of diversity. • *Knowing how to act:* communication, relationship, negotiation, refusal, ethical, and help-seeking skills. 4. **Explain that the adoption of an effective social-emotional/character education program.** • Establishes social-emotional and character education skills as a priority in the school. • Makes it easier for a school to adopt and implement materials consistent with the framework, and reject inconsistent programs. • Gives order and synergy by assuring common threads in materials presented to students. • "When schools implement high-quality SEL programs and approaches effectively, academic achievement…increases…problem behaviors decrease, the relationships that surround each child are improved, and the climate of classrooms and schools changes for the better." (Elias, 2006) 5. **Positive Discipline offers an integrated, comprehensive framework.** • Build the house - For sticky sheet or felt board: move the pieces of the house from the lower half of your fabric to the upper half, starting with the roof. - For power point "build" your schoolhouse starting with the roof using the animation tools (entrance effects). • As you move the pieces explain that this program and the manual provide information and activities for addressing all the important components of an effective social-emotional/character education process/program. It: - Supports academic skill development through the teaching of self-regulation skills and more. - Overlaps with essential pieces of sex education, drug and bullying prevention. - Encourages and provides a process for developing school, family and community partnerships, connections and service learning. - Becomes the framework against which the school can evaluate new program options.

[7] Elias, Maurice J. (2001) adapted from prior versions in: Elias, M. J., Zins, J. E., Weissberg, R. P., Frey, K., Greenberg, M., Haynes, N., Kessler, R., Schwab-Stone, M., & Shriver, T. (1997). Promoting social and emotional learning: Guidelines for educators. Alexandria, VA: Association for Supervision and Curriculum Development.
Elias, M. J., & Clabby, J. F. (1992). Building social problem solving skills: Guidelines from a school-based program. San Francisco: Jossey-Bass.

Directions for Sticky Sheet (a modern replacement for the old felt board):

- Purchase at least a yard of lightweight tent material from a fabric store.
- Go outside and spray one side of the fabric with a quick stick product like Scotch Spray Mount Repositionable Adhesive and follow product directions.
- Fold and store until you need it.
- When posted on the wall or over a chart stand, the sticky sheet creates a convenient way to mount & remove pictures or posters as you talk.

Additional facts and quotes:

- Among the major reasons cited for dropping out of school, several involve social and emotional factors: not getting along with teachers or peers (35.0% and 20.1%, respectively), feeling left out (23.2%), and not feeling safe (12.1%)[11].

- Social-emotional and life skills must be taught explicitly at the elementary and secondary levels. Like reading or math, if social-emotional skills are not taught systematically, they will not be internalized and become part of a child's lifelong repertoire of valued activities. Although this is necessary, CASEL research would suggest it is not sufficient (Elias et al., 1997). Children also benefit from coordinated, explicit, developmentally sensitive instruction in the prevention of specific problems, such as smoking, drug use, alcohol, pregnancy, violence, and bullying. (Elias, 2006)

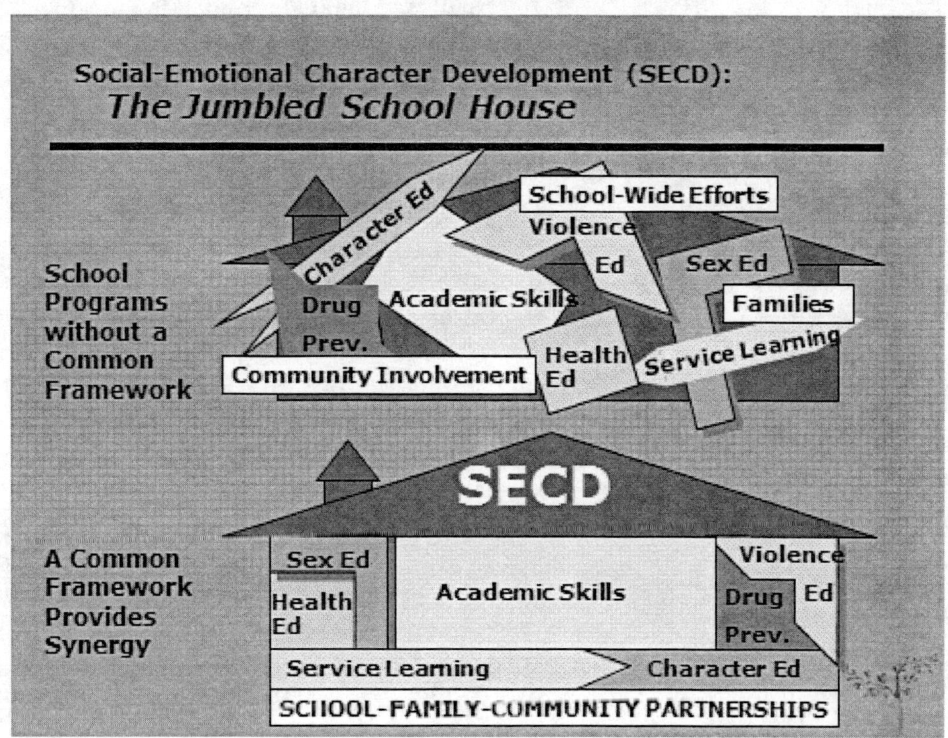

---

11 National Center for Education Statistics. (2002). Dropout rates in the United States 2000. Washington, DC: U.S. Department of Education, Offices of Educational Research and Improvement.

Kindness and Firmness at the Same Time (Grid)

Jody McVittie and Terry Chadsey

Objective:

- To understand that kindness and firmness *at the same time* is very different than trying to balance kindness and firmness.
- To explore the power of connection before correction, its relationship to kindness and firmness, and its impact on effective classroom leadership.

Materials: Flip chart with the grid (beginning and completed samples below).

Comments:

- Social equality means we are all worthy of dignity and respect though we have different roles and responsibilities.
- Democratic environments call for strong leadership.
- The teacher's role is to model and develop leadership in the classroom.
- Limits are most effective when there is follow through that connects before it corrects.
- It's often worth exploring the short-term effects and the long-term effects. For example, kids often enjoy permissiveness—for now. Later on, they discover that they haven't learned what they need to be successful and may feel dependent and angry.

Directions:

1. **Set up**. Explain that the grid is one way of looking at different teaching styles. You can roughly categorize classrooms by their levels of kindness and firmness.
2. **The permissive quadrant**.
   - Ask participants to imagine a classroom (not their own) that has a lot of kindness, but not much firmness.
   - What would you see in the classroom? Scribe in quadrant.
   - What might we call that teaching style? (Permissive, freedom without order.) Write Permissive as the title for this quadrant.
3. **The authoritarian quadrant.**
   - Ask participants to imagine a classroom (not their own) that has a lot of firmness, but not much kindness.
   - What would you see in the classroom? Scribe in quadrant.
   - What might we call that teaching style? (Authoritarian, order with no freedom.) Write Authoritarian as the title for this quadrant.
4. **The neglect quadrant.**
   - Write Neglect as the title for the lower left quadrant.
   - Explain that not many classrooms are missing both firmness and kindness but there are students who live in families without firmness and kindness.
   - There are two general groups of families at high risk for not connecting well with their children:
     - Families that are overwhelmed (divorce, parent ill, homelessness, joblessness, one parent absent, one parent fighting in war, etc.)
     - Families that are busy being busy so that their only time to have connection is in the car
   - Children from families without firmness or kindness may struggle with numerous social and academic skills.
5. **The dance between quadrants.**
   - No teacher does one of these all the time. Most of us struggle to get just the right balance.
   - Putting your marker in the "permissive" quadrant explain that most of us start near here because we want our students to like us.
   - Slide your marker across to the authoritarian quadrant and say, "Until things get out of control and we lay down the law."
   - And we go back and forth desperately trying to balance kindness and firmness. Slide your marker back and forth between the two quadrants.
   - Who controls that dance? The kids usually do; they often find it extremely interesting to experiment with influencing adult behavior.

	6. The democratic/authoritative quadrant. • What might we call that teaching style? (Democratic/Authoritative, order with freedom.) Write Democratic/Authoritative, as the title for this quadrant. • Explain that in Positive Discipline we use kindness and firmness *at the same time.* This eliminates the crazy balancing act. • Explain that this can be a challenge – made worse by language. We often think of kindness as the opposite of firmness. **7. Connection before correction.** • Using your marker cross out the word kindness. Explain that because of how we perceive and use the word kindness it is easier to reframe this as *connection.* • Write connection where the word kindness was. • Pointing to the quadrant, tell participants that this style of teaching is called authoritative or democratic. It is useful to think of it as "connect before correct." • Write Connect B4 Correct in the quadrant.

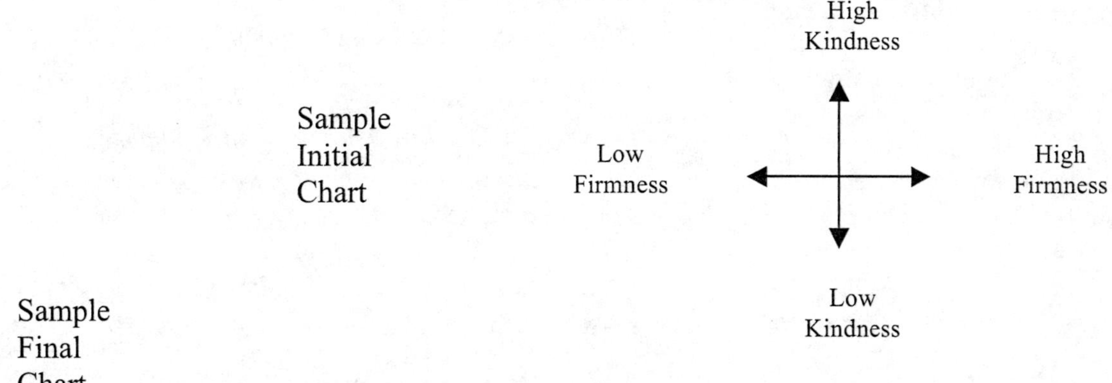

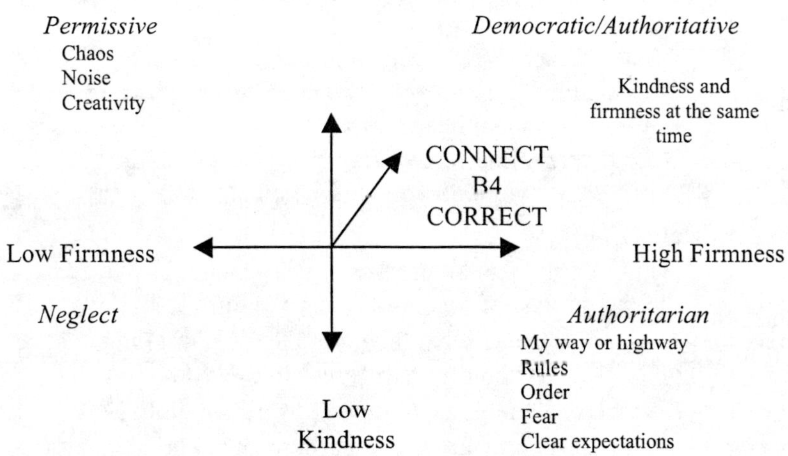

Listening: Effective and Ineffective

From *Teaching Parenting the Positive Discipline Way*, 6th *edition* by Lynn Lott and Jane Nelsen, adapted by Jody McVittie

<table>
<tr>
<td>

Objective:
To experience the difference between effective and ineffective listening.

Materials:
- Flip chart paper
- Markers

Comments:
- The sense of "feeling felt" helps a person regain self-control.
- The sense of "being heard" is so powerful it alone can help us move toward solutions.
- Acknowledging feelings in the "It seems like you feel" statements is a powerful form of connection.

</td>
<td>

Directions:

1. **Set up:**
   - Have audience divide into partners, "A" and "B."
   - Have everyone think of something that they could complain about for 30 seconds. It could be a student's misbehavior or something else that went wrong recently.
2. **First role play:**
   - Post sentence prompt: "I think you should have…."
   - Ask A to complain or rant to B for about 30 seconds.
   - B responds with advice beginning with: "I think you should have…."
3. **Second role play**:
   - Post sentence prompt: "I can't believe you….!"
   - Switch roles. Have B rant to A about something for 30 seconds.
   - A responds with criticism beginning with: "I can't believe you...!"
4. **Third role play:**
   - Post sentence prompt: "It seems like you feel _____because _____ and you wish _____."
   - Maintain the same roles as the second role-play.
   - B will tell the same "rant" again.
   - A responds with effective listening beginning with "It seems like you feel __because __and you wish __." A is then to listen and use only non-verbal communication, regardless of how tempting it is to speak.
   - Explain that the "you wish" part could be funny or serious. Examples:
     - "It *seems like you feel* angry *because* John is bugging you *and you wish* at least for today, he lived on the other side of the moon!"
     - "*It seems like you feel* angry *because* John is bugging you and you *wish* he would stop.
5. **Reflection**
   - This activity can be processed after each role-play, or in the interest of time, only after the third role-play.
   - Ask participants what they were feeling, thinking and deciding in each of the different role-plays.
   - Which style helps them move toward solutions?
   - If it hasn't come up, invite participants to notice that it can feel awkward to criticize other adults, but criticizing children comes more easily.

</td>
</tr>
</table>

Please Be Seated

Adapted from *Positive Discipline in the Classroom Teacher's Guide*, Jane Nelsen and Lynn Lott

Objective: To experience being controlled and to learn what control invites from others. **Materials:** Chairs **Comments:** • We often think control is best until we experience someone trying to control us. • This activity is useful in conjunction with the "Cooperative Juggling" activity to show the contrast between control and cooperation.	**Directions:** 1. **Set up the activity.** • Have the group divide into triads, each group with one chair. • Using a volunteer who is sitting, model the positions: one person sitting, and two behind the chair with hands on the shoulders of the sitting person. • Explain that the job of the sitter will be to stand up. • The job of the standers is to keep the sitter in his/her chair. • You will ask them to rotate about every 30 seconds so everyone has a turn at each position. • Ask them to stay observant. Pay attention to what they are feeling, thinking or deciding as they play the different roles. • *Ask your participants to take care of themselves. If they have neck, shoulder or back problems, ask them to be observers.* 2. **Reflection/process for when they were standing.** After each question, leave room for responses from several participants. • "What were you feeling?" • "What did you notice about your own behavior?" • "What were you deciding about others, about yourself, and about what you would do in the future?" 3. **Reflections/process for when they were sitting.** • What were you feeling?" • "What did you notice about your own behavior?" • "What were you deciding about others, about yourself, and about what you might do in the future? 4. **Taking it further.** • It is powerful to move from here to "Cooperative Juggling" without much discussion, and then compare activities after both are completed. • You can also invite some general reflection on this activity.

The Results of Punishment

From "Punishment" from *Teaching Parenting the Positive Discipline Way 5th edition,* Lynn Lott and Jane Nelsen

<table>
<tr>
<td>

Objective:
To have participants reconnect with their own experience and learning from punishment.

Materials:

- Flip chart for recording
- Results of Punishment Chart (below).

Comments:

- This activity calls common practice into question and often leaves participants asking, "If not punishment, then what?"
- It is helpful to follow this activity immediately with the Solutions vs. Logical Consequences activity found in *Positive Discipline in the School and Classroom Teachers' Guide: Activities for Students*

</td>
<td>

Directions:

1. Set up:

- Ask participants to think of a time when they were punished. It could have been last week, or many years ago.
- Ask them to focus on and remember what they were *feeling, thinking, and deciding* after they were punished.

2. Sharing.

- (Optional) In pairs have them share what they were *feeling, thinking and deciding* as a result of the punishment.
- Divide the flip chart into three columns and write **feeling** at the top of the first column, **thinking** over the top of the second and **deciding** over the top of the third.
- Ask for volunteers to share one at a time what they were feeling, thinking and deciding. This helps everyone understand how what we are feeling and thinking is connected to what we decide.

3. Reflection. Ask the group:

- What did you notice?
- Do you think the outcomes are what the punisher intended?
- Is this what we want students to learn?
- *Comment:* Some participants may say they decided to do something different or not repeat the behavior for which they were punished. Decisions of what not to do (out of fear of getting punished) often result in the person also eliminating behaviors that were not the problem.

  One example is of a participant who reported feeling humiliated after raising her hand and giving an answer that the teacher didn't like. This participant decided to never raise her hand again (and she didn't).

4. Post, review and discuss Jane Nelsen's Results of Punishment chart (below).

</td>
</tr>
</table>

Results of Punishment

Revenge: "They are winning now, but I'll get even"
Resentment: "This is unfair. I can't trust adults"
Rebellion: "I'll show them I can do whatever I want"
Retreat:
Sneaky – "I won't get caught next time" or
Reduced self esteem – "I'm a bad person"

The Results of Rewards

Lois Ingber

Objective:

- To explore the long-term results of rewards.
- To demonstrate that positive incentives and rewards have unappreciated, unintended consequences.
- To recognize rewards do not teach people to do the right thing even when no one is looking.

Materials:

Results of rewards handout

Comments:

- Rewards and punishments erode our relationships with our students. Relationships with our students are our most important tool for *influencing* our students' development.
- Rewards fail to achieve the adult's goal: to encourage a sense of responsibility and accountability in the child, and instead create self-centeredness and loss of mutual respect.
- Rewards are used for control and create hierarchical relationships of superior and inferior.
- Rewards teach people to look for the payoff, rather than doing a task for its own sake.
- Incentives and rewards interfere with creativity and invite shortcuts and cheating.
- Many adults choose rewards or "positive incentives" to control behavior. Though the short-term results may look

Directions:

1. Rewards role-play.

- Ask for a volunteer.
- Stand in front of the person and say, "Pretend I am your spouse or partner." Then say, "I've come up with a new plan! For every night you cook dinner, I'm going to give you a sticker! We'll place the stickers on a chart and at the end of the month, if you fill up the chart, you can have a reward! What would you like it to be?"
- Go with their choice if it is something you agree with, or bargain for an alternative.

2. Process role-play. Ask:

- What were you feeling, thinking and deciding?
- Are you learning how to cook dinner? Are you learning the responsibility of cooking dinner? Why or why not?
- Did you feel respected? What thoughts or decisions are you making about me?
- If the person refused to cooperate (cook dinner in exchange for rewards) ask him/her why he/she refused.

3. Discuss with the group.

- What did you notice?
- What are you learning?

4. Further discussion. These points may come out of the discussion; if not you can bring them out.

- **Rewards distract students from the real issues.** The child becomes more concerned with the reward than learning the *intrinsic value* of the appropriate decision or activity itself.
- **Rewards are manipulative.** When using rewards both the child and adult agree to *be manipulated* and *to manipulate* as they each negotiate to get what they want. Adults think the child receives the reward; the child thinks the opposite: "If you give me what I want, I will reward you with what you want."
- **Rewards and positive incentives teach self-interest** instead of genuine contribution, cooperation and problem solving to meet the needs of the situation. These are key to building community, socially useful behavior, a sense belonging and contribution toward the betterment of the world.
- **Rewards degrade the task.** By making the reward the focus of the plan, the task or chore is cheapened, de-valued or degraded in comparison. It robs students of the opportunity

satisfying, the long-term results are not helpful. • This activity links well with the Praise vs. Encouragement activity or with the Results of Punishment activity or the Laddership to Leadership activity.	to feel capable and responsible for the contribution they can make by doing something important and useful. • **Rewards create a double bind.** - Since the reward is appealing to the student, by accepting the plan the child *agrees* to be placed in an inferior position, relinquishing her dignity and self-respect. - If she does not agree to the plan, thereby retaining her dignity and self-respect, she misses out on something she would enjoy and risks disappointing the adult or making the situation worse for herself by the adult. - She cannot "win" in either scenario. • **Rewards decrease respect.** Rewards create a top-down (superior/inferior) relationship and as a result the child loses respect for both the adult and herself. • **Rewards are confusing.** Because all of this occurs out of awareness it is difficult for students (or adults) to sort out what is actually going on. **5. Give handout** "The Results of Rewards" and discuss.

Extension (based on an example in *Punished by Rewards* by Alfie Kohn):
Rewards role-play 2.

- Ask for another volunteer.
- Stand in front of him/her and say, "If I give you $100, would you take off your shoes?"
- If they do it, pretend handing them the money.
- If they don't agree but ask for more money, agree to it.

Process role – play 2

- What were you feeling, thinking and deciding?
- Did I teach you to take off your shoes? Why or why not?
- Did you feel respected? What thoughts or decisions are you making about me?
- If the person refused to cooperate ask him/her why he/she refused.

The Results of Rewards Handout

Lois Ingber

Teachers want their students to behave and often choose to use rewards or positive incentives as a replacement for punishment. Some teachers use both rewards and punishments. We propose that neither *rewards* nor *punishments* are helpful in teaching our students to become ethical, caring responsible adults. Why do we say this?

1. Rewards and punishments are two sides of the same coin: they both aim to *control* behavior instead of focusing on *teaching*. Rewards and punishment model the use of *power* as a means of solving problems.
2. Rewards and punishments are forms of *"doing to" and "doing for"* students instead of *"doing with"* students. They don't invite students to learn from within or teach cooperative problem solving, both necessary skills in today's world.
3. Rewards and punishments *distract* students from the *real* issues. The child becomes more concerned with avoiding the punishment or gaining the reward than learning the *intrinsic value* of the appropriate decision or activity itself.
4. Rewards and punishments erode our *relationships* with our students. Relationships with our students are our most important tool for *influencing* our students' development.

Rewards:

- **Eventually lose their effectiveness.** The child loses interest in "working for" the reward, or may want rewards that are more appealing (bigger, better).
- **May bring temporary "obedience,"** but never help a child develop a commitment to a task or action when there is no "payoff."
- **Teach students to be self-centered.** They learn to think, "What's in it for me?" instead of doing the activity simply because it is worth doing for its own sake.
- **Are discouraging.** They are conditioned on the successful completion of the task. *Without successful completion, the withholding of the reward turns it into a "punishment" because; from the child's perspective the child is denied something promised.*
- **Erode intrinsic motivation.** The child does not have the opportunity to develop an interest or liking in the activity on its own merits. Students are denied the opportunity to make a genuine contribution, the foundation for feeling responsible and capable (belonging and significance).
- **De-value or degrade the task or action needed,** as the "reward" is presented as more important.
- **Interfere with self-esteem.** They create dependency upon an outside person for approval rather than a conscientious evaluation by the child of her own efforts.

Instead of rewards.... focus on solutions with your students:

• Problem solve together. • Share your enjoyment of working together in the classroom. • Avoid making everyday tasks seem like a burden.	• Make agreements and follow through. • Invite the student to contribute to the class by giving him/her a job. • Teach and hold class meetings.

Prepared by Lois Ingber, L.C.S.W., 2008. Sources: *Positive Discipline* by Jane Nelsen and Lynn Lott, and *Unconditional Parenting* and *Punished by Rewards* by Alfie Kohn. Another source with excellent research is *Drive* by Daniel Pink.

Shopping Cart Model of Human Behavior Demonstration

Jody McVittie

Objective:	**Directions:**
• To highlight differences between Adlerian psychology and the behaviorism we see in many schools. • To emphasize that it is more important to teach skills than to offer rewards or consequences. **Materials:** A chair or other moveable piece of furniture. **Comments:** • Misbehavior is a result of lack of skill in regaining belonging and significance. • The misbehavior you see is a solution to another problem that you may not see. • This is a simplification of the models of human behavior but can be helpful to explore the assumptions we've made about behavior.	1. **Set up.** Explain to participants that one way to look at the difference between behaviorism and Adlerian approaches to human behavior is using the "shopping cart demonstration of human behavior." 2. **Shopping cart round 1.** • Hold the chair in front of you pretending it is a shopping cart. Walk forward wiggling it as if it has bad wheels. As you walk offer the explanation below. • Explain: In behaviorism, the belief is that the shopping cart of human behavior has bad wheels. It won't go straight unless you train it by creating "aisles" made up of positive incentives on one side/ negative on the other. The hope is that by the end of the aisle it will have fixed its wheels and have "learned to go straight." 3. **Shopping cart round 2.** • Again hold the chair in front of you pretending it is a shopping cart. Walk straight forward and then mime having hit a little rock at which point the "shopping cart" veers off in one direction. • Explain: The Adlerian model on the other hand, assumes that the wheels are good and that the shopping cart is actually going to go straight, aiming for belonging and significance. It may go off course, like all shopping carts when it hits an obstacle like a pebble that can't be navigated. So it then aims off course until it finds *the skills needed to successfully re-direct toward belonging and significance.*

Six Approaches to Classroom Discipline

Based upon an activity by Mike Brock

Objective:	**Directions**:
• To explore six approaches to discipline from the perspective of the student. • To encourage the use of discipline methods which promote long-term learning for students. **Materials:** • Charts from Two Lists activity • Flip chart paper • 6 Prepared charts (as below) • Markers **Comments:** • There are more options than we realize to address challenges that occur in the classroom. • All solutions are consequences. Not all consequences are solutions. • For a small audience, you might want to reduce the six approaches to four by combining natural and logical consequences as well as prevention and solutions. Just make note of the differences during the presentations.	**1. Set-up.** • Post the lists the group made from the two lists activity at the front of the room. • As a group, choose a simple, common classroom problem experienced on a daily basis, such as students speaking out of turn, interrupting, forgetting to turn in work, etc. • Write the problem on a sheet of chart paper or on the board at the front of the room. • As a group, briefly review each of the discipline methods on the six posted charts. **2. Divide the groups.** • Divide participants into six groups, assigning one chart to each. • Ask each group to fill in both columns of their chart. **3. Review the posters.** • Have each group present and post their completed charts in the following order: - punishment, - rewards, - logical consequences, - natural consequences, - prevention, - solutions. • After each group reads, ask that group: - What's the good news about your approach? - What's the bad news? • Put a star by any student learning that matches something on the list of gifts from the Two Lists activity. **4. Reflection**. Ask participants: • What did you learn from this activity? • What challenges you? • What practices will promote the most long-term learning? • Which practices would you prefer your building leader use with you? • Any other comments?

Create six charts prior to the activity, each with a different title. (List of titles below)

Sample Chart:

6. Looking for Solutions Looking at the problem from the perspective of what can be done to help the student learn to solve it.	
What the Teacher Might Do	What the Student Will Learn

Titles for charts:

1. Punishment: Adult's response to behavior that makes the student "pay" for what he/she has done or failed to do. We often define this as a consequence.

2. Rewards / Reinforcement: Adult's response to behavior that gives something to the student for doing what the adult wants him/her to do.

3. Logical Consequences: Adult's response to behavior is
   - Related to the problem
   - Reasonable
   - Respectful

4. Natural Consequences: Adult's response to behavior is non-action.

5. Prevention: Adults work to prevent the situation in the future.

6. Solutions: Adult's response to behavior that is
   - Related to the problem
   - Reasonable
   - Respectful
   - *AND* Helpful

This includes supporting the student to solve or fix the problem and/or make amends. All solutions are consequences. Not all consequences are solutions.

Storming the Circle

Jody McVittie

Objective:	Directions:
• To understand the power of movement toward belonging. • To gain a deeper understanding that misbehavior is a solution to a different problem (lack of belonging and significance). • To illustrate the importance of teaching social skills to all students (insiders and outsiders). **Materials**: None	1. **Set up the role-play.** • Invite 6-8 participants to form a group by standing in a circle, facing inwards and holding hands. • Invite 2 participants to be "student outsiders" who want to be part of the group. They will do this by "breaking" into the circle and standing in the middle. • Note: At this point, the people in the circle naturally step closer together to tighten their group (develop stronger connection). If this doesn't happen coax them a little. 2. **The role-play**. • Begin by asking the 2 students to make their way into the circle. They can break in however they choose; they just can't hurt anyone. • Stop the role-play after about 30 seconds even if no outsiders have made it "in." 3. **Learning from the first role-play.** • Ask the members of the circle: "What did you notice?" What were you thinking or deciding about yourselves? About the "intruders?" • Ask the student outsiders, "What did you notice?" What were you thinking or deciding about yourselves? About the "members of the circle?" • If an outsider made it into the middle, ask if he/she now successfully feels part of the group? (If no one broke into the middle, ask one of the outsiders to step in before asking.) They usually notice that they still are not connected. 4. **The second role-play.** • Teach the outsiders. Tell them this time they will join the circle instead of breaking into the middle. Suggest that to be more effective they stand next to two people in the circle and ask to be let in. • Before they begin, ask the observers (audience) what would happen if the insiders were unskilled at this point. Would the outsiders be automatically let in? (No) • Teach the insiders briefly by letting them know that as a class you've talked about how to include and welcome people who might be different than you. • Then ask the outsiders to try the more skillful approach. 5. **Learning from the second role-play.** • All are now holding hands in a circle. Ask the former

	insiders what they noticed this time. • Ask the outsiders what they noticed. • Ask everyone to take a deep breath to leave their roles behind, then thank them and invite them to return to their seats. • Ask the observers what they noticed and what they learned watching this activity. **Common observations from participants:** • When kids feel excluded it really invites all sorts of crazy behavior. • Once we (the circle) identified them as aggressive, it was HARD to let them in. • It was easier to let them join than to let them be in the CENTER of the circle. • As kids who don't belong – it seems natural to aim for the center of the circle instead of joining the circle. (Mistaken beliefs!)

They drew a circle that shut me out --
Heretic, rebel, a thing to flout.
But love and I had the wit to win:
We drew a circle that took him in.
-Edwin Markham

"I'm seeing the 'I want to join the circle [behavior]' everywhere I go. Our society doesn't always make it easy to connect. I'm trying to find ways to open the circle in my classroom."

– A Middle School teacher.

Taking Care of Yourself

From "Sometimes I Get so Angry at the Kids I'm Scared" from *Teaching Parenting the Positive Discipline Way, 5th edition* by Lynn Lott and Jane Nelsen, adapted by Jody McVittie and Melanie Miller

Objective:

- To recognize that failure to care for ourselves is hurtful to ourselves and others.
- To recognize the cumulative impact of the stress of daily events.
- To generate and focus on ideas for self-care practices.

Materials:

- Sticky notes (2 per participant)
- Flip chart
- Markers

Comments:

- Taking care of ourselves is essential if we are to do our best with young people.
- We teach better when we feel better.
- It is important to model self-care skills so the young people in our lives can learn them.
- Preview the video referenced below if you plan on including the reference to Steven Covey's rock activity.

Directions:

1. **Set up.**
   - Give each participant 2 sticky notes.
   - Draw a large pot on the flip chart. Make it only big enough to hold about 2/3rds of the sticky notes from participants.
2. **What makes you angry?**
   - Ask participants to write one thing that makes him/her angry on each note.
   - You can offer humorous examples such as: people who blink their lights at me when I am going the speed limit, my mother in law inviting herself to visit when I have other plans.
3. **Filling the pot.**
   - Ask participants to put their sticky note in the pot when they are done writing.
   - Invite participants to share as they walk up or you can read several aloud after some have accumulated.
   - The pot will start to get very full. When participants look for a spot to put their sticky note you might comment, "What happens when a pot gets overfilled?"
4. **The results of our cumulative stress.**
   - Point to the pot of sticky notes and ask, "Is this what your day looks like?"
   - "When these things fill our day and then a student does something really annoying, how are we likely to react?" (Participants usually recognize that the child gets a reaction out of proportion to the incident.)
   - "Do you do your best job as a teacher when you've had a day like this?"
5. **Taking care of yourself.**
   - "What kind of things do you do to take care of yourself?" You will get responses like: exercise, talk to friends, walk pets, listen to music, read, pray, take a hot bath etc.
   - Each time you get a response, move one of the sticky notes from inside the pot to the outside of the pot. Write the response inside the pot where that sticky note was.
   - Gradually instead of a pot filled with sticky notes, you have a pot filled with suggestions of how to take care of yourself. The sticky notes are now stuck on top of each other at the margins of the flip chart and make a powerful visual.

	6. **Reflection** • What did you learn from this? • How do children learn self-care? • What are small steps you could take to improve your self-care? • Time permitting, have participants write down 2 things they will do this week or pair up and share commitments with a partner. 7. **The big rocks (optional).** • Talk about Steven Covey's demonstration[12] of the rocks in the jar. If you take a jar of rocks…all kinds of rocks, big and little and dump them out you will have a pile of rocks. If you then put in all the small rocks, then the medium rocks, and then try to get the big rocks in, what happens? (The big rocks don't fit.) • Ask, "Is taking care of yourself a big rock or a little rock?" "What does that mean for planning your day?"

[12] Video of Steven Covey's rock demonstration: http://www.youtube.com/watch?v=8705cHTKEgQ

Think Tree

Jody McVittie based on work by Wendy Palmer

<table>
<tr>
<td>

Objective:
To embody the sense of kindness and firmness at the same time.

Materials:
None needed

Comment:
• It is important that this activity be modeled with the demonstrator being the one who is pushed before participants work together.
• This activity can be used alone or after teaching styles or a kindness and firmness activity.
• Re-centering into the physical sense of "think tree" can invite students to self-regulate.

</td>
<td>

Directions:
1. **Set the stage.** Briefly review teaching styles with participants:
• Permissive (high freedom, low order)
• Authoritarian (high order, low freedom)
• Democratic/authoritative (high order, high freedom)
2. **Model the activity.** Ask for a volunteer to stand beside you to "play" a little with how different styles feel. S/he will give you a small push on the shoulder as you model each style. (Exaggeration is fun here.)
• *Permissive.*
- Explain that your muscles will be loose.
- When volunteer pushes you move easily away.
• *Authoritarian.*
- Explain you'll be very rigid (feet together, hands tight, muscles rigid).
- When the volunteer pushes you can either lean into him/her (create a power struggle) or be wobbly and unbalanced.
• *Democratic.*
- Explain that in order to be firm and connected you must first connect with yourself. Describe what you are doing as you move into this posture. Put your feet shoulder width apart and feel yourself firmly grounded. Imagine yourself as an oak tree, your legs as the trunk (solid) with deep roots below your feet. As you take another breath, stand tall and let the audience know that the tree also extends upward. When you feel connected and centered, indicate that you are ready for the volunteer to push on your shoulder.
- When the volunteer pushes you, you should feel more centered. Like an oak tree in the wind you may move a tiny bit. If the volunteer pushes too hard, say something like, "I'm new at this so don't give me so much pressure as I'm learning."
3. **Practice.** After the demonstration ask the group to get in pairs and try it themselves. It is helpful to remind them that for the rigid pose they really have to get tight – and for the tree pose to take their time so that they can really feel anchored before they let their partner push.
4. **Reflection.** Invite a discussion.
• What did you notice?
• How did each position feel?
• How did it feel to push on different "styles"?
• What did you learn from this?
5. **Extension** (optional). Some teachers make "think tree" a practice when they enter their room in the morning. They stand in the center of the room, center themselves and then imagine extending a branch of the tree into each corner of the room. Over time, this increases one's ability to be aware of the physical space and the events inside that space.

</td>
</tr>
</table>

The Two Lists: Where Are We and Where Do We Want to Go?

From "What Do You Want for Your Students?" from *Positive Discipline in the Classroom: Teachers Guide* Jane Nelsen and Lynn Lott, adapted by Terry Chadsey and Jody McVittie

Objectives:

- Recognize the importance of social skills for our students.
- Identify skills needed for long-term success.
- Acknowledge common challenges and goals.
- Develop awareness of the importance of practice and role modeling when teaching social skills.

Materials:

Flip chart and markers

Comments:

- This exercise is very effective at the beginning of any introductory talk. It helps participants get in touch with how Positive Discipline will be relevant to them and/or their community.
- Connection to real problems invites buy-in.
- It is helpful to explore and understand what behaviors challenge teachers.
- The list of qualities and gifts is a constant reminder of the long-term goals.

Directions:

1. Brainstorm. Ask participants to brainstorm a list of student challenges and/or behaviors that "push their buttons." Make sure that there is a wide range of challenges and problems listed.

- "Smaller" ones like whining, talking back, not listening and "bigger" ones like violence, drugs, depression, cutting, or anorexia.
- Be sure to add some of the bigger ones if the group has not named them.

2. Tape the list to the wall.

3. Brainstorm again. Start the second list by asking the participants, "What gifts or qualities would you want to give your students by the time they graduate from high school?"

- This list include things like: self-esteem, responsibility, kindness, compassion, faith, problem-solving skills, sense of humor, resilience, love, honesty, ability to form relationships, setting goals, learning from mistakes, communication skills, etc.
- Be sure to add any you think are missing (e.g. sense of humor).
- Point out that this second list rarely includes academic skills.
- Notice that these qualities are what we want in a good neighbor.

4. Tape the list to the wall.

5. Compare the lists. Ask the group to look at the two lists, and with curiosity ask, "How do children learn?" Accept answers until you get one that is "by watching", or "from modeling", or by "doing what you do."

6. Explore. "What do we do when a student does something from the first list?

- Do we model patience, problem solving skills, or a sense of humor?
- Or do we lose it, punish them, or send them out of the classroom?
- What do we do with a student who is missing academic skills (offer support/training), compared to what we do with a student who is missing social skills (exclusion/consequences)?
- How would students learn how to respond appropriately to items on the first list if they didn't see adults modeling appropriate responses? (The "problems" are opportunities to teach)

7. Introduce mirror neurons by doing the "Do as I Say" activity.

8. Review. Our students will learn best from us when we can model what we want from them, even under stress. The Positive Discipline curriculum is what helps move our students and us from the first list to the second list.

9. Save the two lists.

- Some schools post them in the faculty lounge.
- The list of challenges and behaviors is a good reference when looking for problems to use for the Teacher Helping Teacher Problem Solving Steps.

"What" and "How" Questions

Suzanne Smitha

Objectives: • Introduce the concept of "what" and "how" questions. • Help teachers "feel" the different loci of control when "what" and "how" questions are used. • Establish an environment for more effective problem solving. **Materials:** None needed.	**Directions:** **1. Set up.** Ask the audience or a volunteer to: • Put their hands together and • Interlace their fingers. **2. Learn from a volunteer.** Ask one volunteer: • What did you do with your hands? • How did you do it? • Why did you do that with your hands? (The person will answer the "Why" question differently with something like, "Because you told me to.") **3. Learn from the group.** Ask the group: • What did you notice? • How are the "What and How" answers different from the "Why" answer? • Where was the locus of control with each question? (external/internal) **4. Invite discussion** about what students are learning. Bring forward how shifting from why questions to what and how questions helps: - Students assume responsibility for their actions. - The process for effective problem solving. - Open dialogue. - Remove the sense of judgment.

What Are They Learning?

Suzanne Smitha and Jody McVittie

<table>
<tr>
<td>

Objective:
To help teachers become aware of the many life skills students learn from each Positive Discipline lesson.

Materials:
• Flip chart paper
• Markers

Comments:

• Teachers recognize that students learn many life skills from what appears to be a simple lesson.

• The list generated often resembles the list of "gifts" from the Two Lists activity.

• It is useful to keep this list and add to it as new activities are taught.

</td>
<td>

Directions:

1. Set up. Facilitate an activity teachers will use with their own students. Activities that are particularly helpful include: Beginning the Almost Perfect school year, Charlie, Bugs and Wishes, Win/Win, Respecting Differences, Apology of Action. Find them in *Positive Discipline in the School and Classroom Teachers' Guide: Activities for Students.*

2. Deepen the learning. Ask:
• "What are students learning?"
• Scribe answers on a prepared flip chart titled "What are they learning?"
• Repeat and add to the list after each activity.
• Refer to sample list below.

3. Process.
• Ask the group where (during this workshop) have they have seen a similar list? (The Characteristics and Life Skills of the Two Lists activity)
• When these skills are developed, what advantages might students have when approaching academic tasks?

4. Variation.
• This variation can be used following a single activity.
• Draw a circle in the center of the paper.
• In the center of the circle, write the title of the activity, such as "Class Meetings."
• Ask participants, "What are students learning?"
• Attach each response to the circle by writing it on a spoke that juts out from the edge of the circle.
• Follow process in Step 2 above.

</td>
</tr>
</table>

Sample list:

I am not alone
Others feel like I do
I can help others
How to listen
My classmates care
How to make amends
Cooperation
We have different opinions
Others have good ideas
How to ask for what I want
Problem solving skills
We are all responsible
Respect for others
We see the world differently

The Wright Family

Cheryl Forse, Deb Pysno, Catherine Bronnert, and Dori Keiper

<table>
<tr>
<td>

Objective:

- Enhance awareness of how stress impacts one's ability to process information.
- Increase awareness of the kinds of stressors students experience and the impact this has on learning.

Materials:

- 1 to 3 small objects for each participant. (coins, buttons, stones, candy, etc.)
- The Life with the Wright Family Story (attached below)

Comments:

- We are naturally wired to seek belonging and significance. Students who do not have an inherent sense of belonging and significance experience stress as they move toward finding their place and sense of value.
- When stress is increased due to academic, social or behavioral challenges, a student's ability to attend to content is significantly compromised.

</td>
<td>

Directions:

1. Set-up.

- Invite all participants to form a circle: each standing close enough to reach the hand of the people beside them.
- Distribute up to 3 objects to each person.
- Ask them to listen to the story you are about to read.
- When they hear the word "right," they are to pass an object to the person on their right. When they hear the word "left", they pass an object to the person on their left.

2. Read the Wright Family Story.

- Read the complete story at a steady normal pace.
- Continue even if there is chaos, confusion and participants are dropping objects.
- When done reading, ask participants to "freeze" and hold onto any object/s in their hand.

3. Ask curiosity questions.

- Ask the questions listed below the story.

4. Reflection on activity.

- What happened?
- What were you thinking and feeling?
- What decisions did you make during the process?
- What did you notice?
- What did you learn?

5. Connection to the classroom.

- How does this relate to learning in a classroom? (When we shift our focus from one thing to another, we are less efficient learners.)
- What kinds of stressors impact students' ability to process and integrate information? (Belonging and significance, family, peers, safety, etc.)

</td>
</tr>
</table>

Extension/Variation:

- Prior to starting this activity, ask the group to brainstorm a list of "life stressors." (Morning rush, busy schedules, paying bills, relationships, jobs/responsibilities, etc.)
- Begin the activity as in step one.
- After giving each participant their small object/s, ask them to reflect for a moment, making a connection between their held object/s and their own personal life stressors.
- Continue with directions above.

Reflection: In addition to the questions and reflection above, make a connection to how we all have life stressors, yet how we carry and handle these may be different.

- Who gave all their object/s and stressors away? Who held onto their object/s and stressors?
- Who gave up on the process and didn't want to deal with their object/s and stressors?
- Who gave all their focus to the object/s and stressors?

Story: This activity was done with a K-8 school staff. After the middle school teachers did this activity with their students, the students then went to the lower school classrooms and did the activity with the 2nd graders. When the older students returned, they asked to see the staff's list of stressors. They had made the connection that student and adult stressors were very similar.

Life with the Wright Family Story[13]

One day the Wright family decided to take a vacation. The first thing they had to decide was who would be left at home, since there was not enough room in the Wright family car for all of them. Mr. Wright decided that Aunt Linda Wright would be the one left at home. Of course, this made Aunt Linda Wright so mad that she left the house immediately, yelling, "It will be a right cold day before I return!"

The Wright family now bundled up the children – Tommy Wright, Susan Wright, Timmy Wright and Shelly Wright, and got into the car and left. Unfortunately, as they turned out of the driveway, someone had left a trashcan in the street, so they had to turn right around and stop the car. They told Timmy Wright to get out of the car and move the trash can so they could get going. Timmy took so long that they almost left him in the street. Once the Wright family got on the road, Father Wright wondered if he had left the stove on. Mother Wright told him not to worry, as she had checked the stove and he had not left it on. As they turned right at the corner, everyone started to think about other things that they might have left undone.

No need to worry now, they were off on a right fine vacation. When they arrived at the gas station, Mother Wright put gas in the car and then discovered that she had left her wallet at home. So, Tommy Wright ran home to get the money that was left behind. After Tommy left, Susan Wright started to feel sick. She left the car, saying that she had to throw up. This, of course, got Father Wright's attention and he left the car in a hurry. Shelly Wright wanted to watch Susan get sick, so she left the car, too. Mother Wright was left with Timmy Wright, who was playing a game in the backseat.

With all of this going on, Father Wright decided that this was not the right time to take a vacation, so he gathered up all of the family and left the gas station as quickly as he could. When he arrived home, he turned left into the driveway and said, "I wish the Wright family had never left home today!"

Questions:

1. Why was Aunt Linda Wright unable to come on the trip? (Not enough room in the car)
2. How many children did the Wright family have? (4)
3. Who moved the trashcan? (Timmy)
4. What did Mr. Wright worry about at home? (The stove)
5. Why did Susan leave the car? (She started to feel sick)
6. Who went back home to get Mother Wright's wallet? (Tommy)
7. Where was Timmy at the gas station? (In the backseat of the car)

---

13 This story is available from multiple sources on the Internet. The original source is not clear.

Resources

Adverse Child Experience (ACE) Study. Retrieved from www.acestudy.org

Albert, Linda (2003). *Cooperative discipline.* Circle Pines, Minnesota: AGS.

Bireda, Martha R. (2010). *Cultures in conflict: Eliminating racial profiling*, (5th ed). Lanham, Maryland: Rowman and Littlefield Education.

Bettner, Betty Lou, Ed. (1989). *An adlerian resource book.* Chicago: NASAP.

Blum, R.W. & Rinehart P.M. (1998). Reducing the risk: Connections that make a difference in the lives of youth. Retrieved from http://casel.org/publications/reducing-the-risk-connections-that-make-a-difference-in-the-lives-of-youth.

Cole, Susan F., O'Brien, Jessica Greenwald, Gadd, M. Geron, Ristuccia, Joel, Wallace, D. Luray, Gregory, Michael. (2005). *Massachusetts Advocates for Children: Helping Traumatized Children Learn.* Retrieved from http://www.massadvocates.org/download-book.php

College of Education, The Ohio State University. (2003). Classroom management in a diverse society. *Theory into Practice,* Volume 42, No. 4.

Davies, Anne, Cameron, Caren, Politano, Colleen, & Gregory, Kathleen. (1992). *Together is better: Collaborative assessment, evaluation and reporting.* Winnipeg, Canada: Peguis.

Davis, Penny G. The impact of abuse and neglect on attachment, brain development, learning and behavior. DVD available from www.respectful-relationships2.com

Deiro, J. (2003). Do your students know you care? *Educational Leadership* 60(6), 60-63.

Dreikurs, Rudolf. (1964). *Children: The challenge.* New York: Hawthorn Books, Inc.

Dreikurs, Rudolf. (1971). *Social equality: The challenge of today.* Chicago: Adler School of Professional Psychology.

Dweck, Carol S. (2006). *Mindset: The new psychology of success.* New York: Random House.

Dweck, Carol. http://nymag.com/news/features/27840/

Elias, Maurice J. (2001) adapted from prior versions in: Elias, M. J., Zins, J. E., Weissberg, R. P. Frey, K., Greenberg, M., Haynes, N., Kessler, R., Schwab-Stone, M., & Shriver, T. (1997). *Promoting social and emotional learning: Guidelines for educators.* Alexandria, VA: Association for Supervision and Curriculum Development and Elias, M. J., & Clabby, J. F. (1992). *Building social problem solving skills: Guidelines from a school-based program.* San Francisco: Jossey-Bass.

Elias, Maurice J. (2006). The connection between academic and social emotional learning. In Elias, Maurice J. and Arnold, Harriett, *The Educator's Guide to Emotional Intelligence and Academic Achievement.* Thousand Oaks, CA: Corwin Press

Evans, T. (1996). Encouragement: The key to reforming classrooms. *Educational Leadership* 54(1), 81-85.

Felitti, Vincent J. (2002). The relationship of adverse childhood experiences to adult health: Turning gold into lead. (English translation from: Felitti VJ. Belastungen in der Kindheit und Gesundheit im Erwachsenenalter: die Verwandlung von Gold in Blei. *Z psychsom Med Psychother* 2002; 48(4): 359-369). Retrieved from http://www.acestudy.org/files/Gold_into_Lead-_Germany1-02_c_Graphs.pdf

Goertz, Donna Bryant. (2001). *Children who are not yet peaceful: Preventing exclusion in the early elementary classroom.* Berkley, CA: Frog Ltd.

Greene, Ross. (2008). *Lost at school: Why our kids with behavioral challenges are falling through the cracks and how we can help them.* New York, NY: Scribner.

Greenwald O'Brien, Jessica P., and Burnett, Laurie, Editors. (2008). *Teachers' strategies guide for working with children exposed to trauma* (3rd ed.). Framingham, MA: self-published.

Ingber, L., & McVittie, J. (2007). *BRIDGES: Building relationships for improved discipline, academic gains and effective schools.* Self Published

Inlay, L. (2003). Values: The implicit curriculum. *Educational Leadership,* 60(6), 69-71.

Institute for American Values. (2003). *Hardwired to connect: The new scientific case for authoritative communities.* Executive Summary retrieved from http://www.americanvalues.org/ExSumm-print.pdf

Krakovsky, Marina. (2007). The effort effect. *The Stanford Magazine*, May/June 2013. Retrieved from http://www.stanfordalumni.org/news/magazine/2007/marapr/features/dweck.html

Learning First Alliance. (2001). Every child learning: Safe and supportive schools. *Association for Supervision and Curriculum Development*. Retrieved from http://www.learningfirst.org/publications/safeschools/

Lott, Lynn, Inter, Riki, & Mendenhall, Barbara. (1999). *Do-it-yourself therapy: How to think, feel, and act like a new person in just 8 weeks.* Franklin Lakes, NJ: Career Press.

Lott, Lynn, & Nelsen, Jane. (1998). *Teaching parenting the positive discipline way: A step-by-step approach to starting and leading parenting classes* (5th ed.). United States: Empowering People.

Lott, Lynn, & Nelsen, Jane. (2008). *Teaching parenting the positive discipline way: A step-by-step approach to starting and leading parenting classes* (6th ed.). United States: Empowering People.

McKay, Gary, McKay, Joyce, Eckstein, Daniel, Maybell, Steven. (2001). *Raising respectful kids in a rude world.* Roseville, CA: Prima Publishing.

McVitte, Jody. Challenge of the week: 2 X 10. Retrieved from http://hostedp0.vresp.com/634436/2c5da0bea8/ARCHIVE

Medea, Andrea. (2004). *Conflict unraveled: Fixing problems at work and in families*. Chicago: PivotPoint Press.

National Center for Education Statistics. (2002). Dropout rates in the United States 2000. Washington, DC: U.S. Department of Education, Offices of Educational Research and Improvement.

Nelsen, Jane. (2006). *Positive discipline*. United States: Ballantine Books.

Nelsen, Jane. (1997). *Positive discipline in the classroom teacher's guide: A step-by-step approach to bring positive discipline to the classroom and to help teachers of all grade levels implement classroom meetings* (Revised Edition). United States: Empowering People.

Nelsen, Jane, and Erwin, Cheryl. *Positive discipline for single parents: Facilitator's Guide*. United States: Empowering People.

Nova Science Now. (1.25.05). Mirror Neurons. Retrieved from http://www.pbs.org/wgbh/nova/body/mirror-neurons.html

Perry, Bruce D. (2001). Consequences of emotional neglect in childhood, adapted in part from: *Maltreated children: Experience, brain development and the next generation.* New York: W.W. Norton & Company, in preparation. Retrieved from http://www.childtrauma.org/images/stories/Articles/attcar4_03_v2_r.pdf

Perry, Bruce. (2009) Examining child maltreatment through a neurodevelopmental lens: Clinical applications of the neurosequential model of therapeutics. *Journal of loss and Trauma*, 14:240-255, 2009. Retrieved from http://www.childtrauma.org/images/stories/Articles/traumaloss_bdp_final_7_09.pdf

Pink, Daniel on TED: The Science of Motivation http://www.ted.com/talks/dan_pink_on_motivation.html

Pink, Daniel H. (2009). *Drive: The surprising truth about what motivates us*. New York, NY: Riverhead Books. RSA on Daniel Pink's *Drive*: http://www.youtube.com/watch?v=u6XAPnuFjJc

Resnick, M.D., Bearman, P.S., Blum, R.W, Buoman, K.E., Harris, K.M., Jones, J., . . . and Udry, J.R. (1997). Protecting adolescents from harm: Findings from the national longitudinal study on adolescent health. *Journal of the American Medical Association*, 278 (10), 823 – 832.

Rightmyer, Elizabeth Campbell. (2003). Democratic discipline: Children creating solutions. *Young Children,* July, 38-45.

Saphier, Jon, Haley-Speca, Mary Ann and Grower, Robert. (2008). *The skillful teacher* (6th ed.). Acton, MA: Research for Better Teaching

Schaps, E. (2003). Creating a school community. *Educational Leadership* 60 (6), 31-33.

Siegel, Daniel J. (2010). Dr. Daniel Siegel presenting a hand model of the brain. Retrieved from http://www.youtube.com/watch?v=DD-lfP1FBFk

Siegel, Daniel J., & Hartzell, Mary. (2003). *Parenting from the inside out: How a deeper self-understanding can help you raise children who thrive.* New York: Jeremy P. Tarcher = Putnam.

Sugai, G, Sprague, J.R, Horner, R.H., Walker, H.M. (2000). Preventing school violence: The use of office discipline referrals to assess and monitor school-wide discipline interventions. *Journal of Emotional and Behavioral Disorders*, 8 (2), 94 – 101.

Taylor, John F. (1984). *Person to person: Awareness techniques for counselors, group leaders, and parent educators*. Saratoga, California: R & E Publishers.

Tough, Paul. (2012). *How children succeed: Grit, curiosity and the hidden power of character.* New York, NY: Houghton Mufflin.

Wang, M. C., Haertel, G. D., & Walberg, H. J. (1997).Toward a knowledge base for school learning. *Review of Educational Research*, 63, 249–294.

Weissberg, Roger P., and Durlak, Joseph A. (2011) The impact of enhancing students' social and emotional learning: A meta-analysis of school based universal interventions. Retrieved from http://casel.org/why-it-matters/benefits-of-sel/meta-analysis Full text retrieved from: http://onlinelibrary.wiley.com

www.positivediscipline.com for free online newsletter from Jane Nelsen as well as all Positive Discipline books, manuals, materials and workshops.

www.positivediscipline.org Website of the Positive Discipline Association. A 501 C 3 non profit supporting respectful relationships in homes, schools and communities, for Teleconferences, workshops, resources and information.

www.SoundDiscipline.org Website for Newsletter for the 501 C 3 non profit Sound Discipline.

Teresa LaSala, a Certified Positive Discipline Lead Trainer, provides training, consultation and supportive services in public, private, charter and parochial schools throughout the United States and internationally. She has been a member of the Positive Discipline Association's Board of Directors since 2004 and regularly facilitates Positive Discipline in the Classroom and Parenting with Positive Discipline workshops and certification trainings.

Teresa is a Whole Child Faculty Member - Regional Specialist for ASCD (an educational leadership organization). She serves as a School Culture and Climate Field Consultant with The United Way of Northern New Jersey's Youth Empowerment Alliance Program and has received an award from the New Jersey State Department of Education, as part of a team, for implementing a "Role Model Character Education Program" (based on the Positive Discipline Whole School Model). She is a licensed nurse with 23 years of experience in the areas of family and pediatric care, child development, and general medicine. Teresa resides in Denville, New Jersey with her husband Jim and two daughters, Meaghan and Lauren, who have been her greatest joy and teachers.

Jody McVittie is a Certified Positive Discipline Lead Trainer who has been teaching Positive Discipline in the Classroom since 1994. She has consulted for dozens of schools: public, independent, early childhood, elementary, and secondary. Her work with schools includes trainings in Spanish (Nicaragua) for First Nations Communities (in northern British Columbia) and for a school for the deaf. She is currently the Director of Program for Sound Discipline.

Jody received her medical degree from Case Western University and completed a family medicine residency and a fellowship in Modesto California before returning to the Pacific Northwest to practice medicine. More recently she has shifted her focus to broader community issues that impact health outcomes including parenting, education, trauma and the impact of intra-family violence. In 2012, she was honored by the Center for Ethical Leadership with the Bill Grace Legacy award. Jody lives in Seattle, Washington and is the mother of three young adults who have been some of her best teachers.

Suzanne Smitha is a Certified Positive Discipline Lead Trainer who has used Positive Discipline with schools and families since 1991. She earned an M.S. degree from the University of Tennessee and continued advanced studies in North Carolina where she now lives. She served as a licensed school psychologist in a large urban school district for over 35 years, retiring in 2009. She currently works as an educational consultant, providing consultation and training for staffs of public, private, charter and parochial schools as well as parenting education classes in her community. She enjoys travel to be with her two adult daughters and her two grandchildren. Suzanne served for many years on the board of the Positive Discipline Association, and currently volunteers with community agencies and boards.